how2become

GCSE Maths is Easy

www.How2Become.com

As part of this product, you have also received FREE access to online tests that will help you to pass GCSE Maths.

To gain access, simply go to:

www.MyEducationalTests.co.uk

Get more products for passing any test or interview at:

www.How2Become.com

Orders: Please contact How2become Ltd, Suite 14, 50 Churchill Square Business Centre, Kings Hill, Kent ME19 4YU.

You can order through Amazon.co.uk under ISBN 9781910602133, via the website www.How2Become.com or Gardners.com.

ISBN: 9781910602133

First published in 2015 by How2become Ltd.

Updated in 2018.

Typeset for How2Become Ltd by Anton Pshinka.

DISCLAIMER

Every effort has been made to ensure that the information contained within this guide is accurate at the time of publication. How2Become Ltd is not responsible for anyone failing any part of any selection process as a result of the information contained within this guide. How2Become Ltd and their authors cannot accept any responsibility for any errors or omissions within this guide, however caused. No responsibility for loss or damage occasioned by any person acting, or refraining from action, as a result of the material in this publication can be accepted by How2Become Ltd.

The information within this guide does not represent the views of any third party service or organisation.

CONTENTS

INTRODUCTION

INTRODUCTION TO YOUR NEW GUIDE

Welcome to your new guide, *GCSE Maths is Easy*. This guide is a comprehensive testing book which provides lots of sample questions for you to work through.

The book is aimed at anyone who wishes to successfully pass a mathematical test, whether that be pupils sitting GCSE Maths, or adults undergoing job application processes.

The key to success for mathematical testing books is practice and preparation. Try your hardest to get 100% in your answers. Aiming for 100% will enable you to achieve success far more likely than if you sit a test in a negative frame of mind.

We have purposely supplied you with lots of questions in order for you to gain a complete understanding of what you are likely to face in such tests. It is important that when working through this book, you check your answers. Knowing where you went wrong and what you need to do differently is just as important in terms of successfully completing mathematical tests. If you know how to fix your mistakes, you are more likely to get the answer correct next time.

STRUCTURE OF THE BOOK

This book follows a very simple structure in order for you to make the most out of the guide. We have provided a variety of testing sections, each with a variety of questions and levels of difficulty for you to work through. Work through each chapter and then check your answers to see how well you are doing.

This comprehensive *GCSE Maths is Easy* testing guide follows the structure as formulated below:

- Introduction – introducing your new guide

- About Maths is Easy

- 24 sections of mathematical concepts including:

    o Fractions
    o Decimals
    o Percentages
    o Ratios
    o Statistics
    o Brain Teasers
    o Areas
    o Bearings
    o And many other mathematical formulas.

- A Few Final Words

ABOUT GCSE
MATHS IS EASY

The sole purpose of this book is simple – to make maths easy! In order to successfully pass any mathematical test, it is important to get to grips with the basic arithmetic. This book has been specifically designed with the intention to create a guide that is easy to follow, provides detailed explanations, example questions, and practice questions for you to work through at a pace that suits you.

This book uses some **unusual methods** to explain mathematics; you may not have come across these methods before; but we have used these methods in our guide to demonstrate that they **actually** work! The first step in any learning process is to have some understanding of what to do and how to do it. We have made it our fundamental aim to assure you of methods and formulas that guarantee correct answers, as well as easy execution.

This book is all about doing things! After reading detailed explanations on a particular mathematical area, you will be asked to complete a series of questions, asked to think about certain things; it is all about making you active, so you fully comprehend how to achieve the correct answers.

The chapters on different arithmetics can be done in any order, but is considered most beneficial if you complete the chapters in order of appearance in the book. The book has been carefully laid out to ensure each stage of mathematical knowledge and understanding is reached, before moving on to a different, and slightly harder chapter.

Use these methods to learn how to complete mathematical equations and build your confidence in relation to any math problem!

Maths made interesting!

This book is all about realism. It uses fun and interesting facts for you to understand maths in a way that makes it more compelling to learn. You will come across questions in relation to:

- Car rallies to solve maps;
- Sunken treasure ships for you to locate;
- The secrets of mazes and a whole range of other interesting facts.

This book provides detailed techniques and formulas that have been carefully broken down and explained, in order to provide a thorough and easy account of how to solve mathematical equations. These techniques are ways in which maths can be easily solved, and by using these techniques will help simplify maths that you once found difficult to complete.

What you'll need

In order to successfully complete the questions in this guide, there are a few things that might be of particular use to you:

1. A calculator (we advise you try the questions without a calculator to better your arithmetic). If however, you are particularly stuck on a question, a calculator may help you. Feel free to use a calculator when checking your answers.
2. A compass.
3. A protractor.
4. A ruler.
5. A set square.

Finally, we have also provided you with some additional **FREE** online psychometric tests which will help to further improve your competence in this particular testing area. To gain access, simply go to:

www.MyPsychometricTests.co.uk

Good luck and best wishes,

The how2become team

The How2Become Team

CHAPTER 1

What is a Fraction?

1. WHAT IS A FRACTION?

The dictionary tells us that a fraction is a "small piece" or a "scrap". Unfortunately these "small pieces" can all be different sizes.

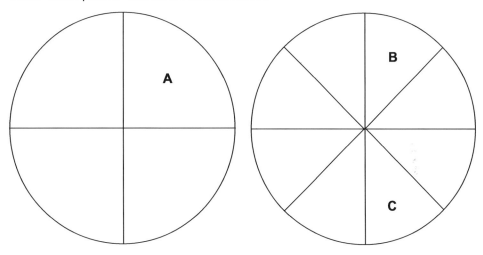

These questions rely on common sense. There is nothing mysterious about fractions!

Look at the examples above.

Piece A is 1 piece
The shape has been cut into 4 **equal** pieces.

Piece A is $\frac{1}{4}$

Piece B is 1 piece
The shape has been cut into 8 **equal** parts.

Piece B is $\frac{1}{8}$

Pieces B and C are two pieces
The shape has been cut into 8 **equal** pieces.

Pieces B and C together are $\frac{2}{8}$

It's as simple as that. Fractions are just shorthand.
Shorthand is the name given to anything that helps people to write faster.

So $\frac{2}{6}$ is just shorthand for "cut something up into 6 equal parts, and take 2 of the pieces".

It's a good job you don't have to write long sentences like that every time. It is much easier to write $\frac{3}{4}$ than it is to write "cut something up into 4 **equal** pieces, and take 3 of the pieces". But they both mean exactly the same thing.

$\frac{1}{5}$ is shorthand for "cut something up into 5 **equal** pieces, and take 1 of the pieces".

$\frac{5}{12}$ is shorthand for "cut something into 12 **equal** pieces, and take 5 of the pieces".

Mathematicians are lazy and often use shorthand. Now, using shorthand has become so used, that everyone uses shorthand writing.

Here is something written in 3 different ways.

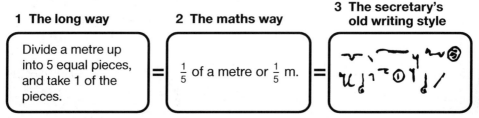

1 The long way	**2 The maths way**	**3 The secretary's old writing style**
Divide a metre up into 5 equal pieces, and take 1 of the pieces.	$\frac{1}{5}$ of a metre or $\frac{1}{5}$ m.	

These 3 ways might look different but they all mean the same thing.

Fractions occur all the time. We have all heard of half an hour ($\frac{1}{2}$ hr) or a quarter of a kilogram ($\frac{1}{4}$ kg).

What actual thing could $\frac{1}{7}$ be talking about?

First, remember what $\frac{1}{7}$ is shorthand for.
"Cut something up into 7 **equal** pieces, and take 1 of the pieces".

It could be talking about a day, because if a week is cut into 7 **equal** pieces, then each piece represents 1 day.
$\frac{2}{7}$ could be talking about 2 days.

What else could $\frac{2}{7}$ be talking about?

2 of the 7 Deadly Sins or 2 of the 7 Seas.Normally we use fractions without thinking about what they may be talking about.

Exercise 1

1. What could these fractions be talking about? There may be more than one answer to some of them.

   a) $\dfrac{1}{24}$ $\dfrac{9}{24}$ d) $\dfrac{1}{60}$ $\dfrac{7}{60}$

   b) $\dfrac{1}{100}$ $\dfrac{17}{100}$ e) $\dfrac{1}{10}$ $\dfrac{7}{10}$

   c) $\dfrac{3}{52}$ $\dfrac{13}{52}$ f) $\dfrac{11}{30}$ (think about months)

When you have completed these questions, check your answers and make sure you understand how the fractions are working, before attempting the next set of questions.

Now, there are some sentences in maths that are written as shorthand. They look very strange. Turn them into ordinary English by writing them without any fractions. <u>The first one is started for you.</u>

2. You go along for a job. The boss says, "Each week you will work $\frac{5}{7}$ of a week, $\frac{8}{24}$ of each day with $\frac{1}{24}$ of each day for dinner."

   $\frac{5}{7}$ of a week means 5 days (because $\frac{1}{7}$ of a week is one day). Therefore the beginning of the answer is:

   "Each week you will work 5 days…"

3. You have just taken your shoes to be re-heeled. The shop owner says, "Can you wait a bit? It will take about $\frac{1}{3}$ of an hour."

4. The person in the ticket office said "You need £$\frac{7}{10}$ of a pound change."

5. The card player said "I have only got $\frac{8}{52}$ of a pack and I should have $\frac{9}{52}$ of a pack. Someone has got $\frac{1}{52}$ of a pack up their sleeve."

6. "I am out of training", said the athlete. "It will probably take me $\frac{25}{60}$ of a minute."

It is easy to see that $\frac{7}{7}$ could be talking about a whole week, or $\frac{52}{52}$ could be talking about a whole pack of cards.

Big numbers don't make any difference. $\frac{3,572}{3,572}$ minutes still means 1 whole minute.

$\frac{3,572}{3,572}$ minutes means "cut a minute up into 3,572 **equal** pieces, and take 3,572 of the pieces." In other words, take **ALL** of the pieces. (A bit of a waste of time cutting it up in this case!)

Certain problems can now be worked out.

When a lorry was $\frac{1}{5}$ full it carried 2 tonnes. How much could it carry when it was completely full?

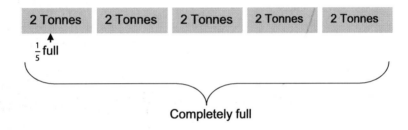

In this case the fraction is $\frac{1}{5}$ and you know that it will take 5 of these ($\frac{5}{5}$) to be a whole lorry full. Of course, you can just work it out, but see how a picture helps to make things clearer.

Interesting TRUE facts

A $\frac{1}{4}$ of the fleas removed from a red squirrel came to 3,000. How many fleas did the squirrel have altogether?

$\quad$ A $\frac{1}{4}$ $\qquad$ = 3,000 fleas

$\quad$ A $\frac{1}{4}$ $\qquad$ = 3,000 fleas

$\quad$ A $\frac{1}{4}$ $\qquad$ = 3,000 fleas

$\quad$ A $\frac{1}{4}$ $\qquad$ = 3,000 fleas

$\quad$ ————————————

$\quad$ 1 squirrel = 12000 fleas

Exercise 2

1. A $\frac{1}{5}$ of the way up the Sears Roebuck skyscraper in Chicago is 22 floors. How many floors are there altogether?

2. In the deepest dive with one breath, $\frac{1}{4}$ of the way down was 86 feet. How deep was the dive?

3. $\frac{1}{10}$ of the passengers in a Jumbo jet is 50. How many passengers can the jet carry when it is full?

4. 2,000 years ago, $\frac{1}{11}$ of an average man's life was 3 years. How long did an average man live?

5. At the same time, $\frac{1}{9}$ of an average woman's life was 3 years. How long did an average woman live?

6. In the Congo in 1950, $\frac{1}{3}$ of the average person's life was 13 years. How long did these people live?

7. Some South American Indians use poison from a particular frog to put on the tips of their arrows. It is one of the world's most dangerous poisons and $\frac{1}{1000000}$ of a gram would kill someone. How many people would 1 gram kill?

8. The world's most expensive perfume is De Beren's Number 1. It costs £66.66 for $\frac{1}{3}$ of an ounce. How much does 1 ounce cost?

9. A $\frac{1}{5}$ of an ounce of gold would cost £147. How much would 1 ounce cost?

How Full is the Jar?

This jar is 60 mm tall. It has some fluid in it.
How full would you say it is?

It is clearly less than $\frac{1}{2}$ full. Is it $\frac{1}{4}$ full, or maybe $\frac{1}{3}$ full, or $\frac{2}{5}$ full?
There must be a way of finding out.

Carefully measure the height of fluid. It comes to 18mm.

There are 60 mm to the top of the jar so the jar is $\frac{18}{60}$ full.

This is because the jar is broken up into 60 **equal** parts (each 1mm) and the fluid reaches the 18 mm mark.

How **easy** is that?

We wouldn't leave the answer as $\frac{18}{60}$ – even though it is correct.

The answer can be made much simpler to understand and we will come back to this once we look at simplifying fractions.

Turning Fractions into Easier Fractions

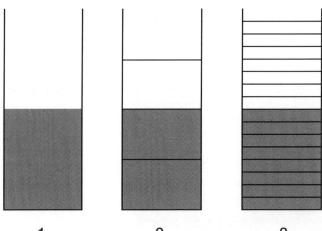

$$\frac{1}{2} \quad = \quad \frac{2}{4} \quad = \quad \frac{8}{16}$$

All the above fractions are the same. They all amount to a half. In the last case, you cut the shape up into 16 **equal** pieces, and take 8 of them. But that means you still have half of the shape.

Fractions which are the same but look different (like $\frac{1}{2}$ and $\frac{13}{26}$) are called **EQUIVALENT FRACTIONS**. 'Equivalent' is just a word that means the 'same as'.

- $\frac{1}{2}$, $\frac{2}{4}$ and $\frac{13}{26}$ are all the same amount (equivalent) but $\frac{1}{2}$ is the easiest to understand.

- $\frac{1}{3}$ and $\frac{2}{6}$ are the same amount (equivalent) but $\frac{1}{3}$ is the easiest to understand.

It is a good idea to turn fractions into easier ones (if possible) because, it can make calculations a lot easier. This is called **SIMPLIFYING FRACTIONS**.

<u>What we need is a way of going about it.</u>

Can $\frac{12}{30}$ be made easier? Here is the way to try:

- Start with the number 2 and ask "will it go into both the top number and the bottom number?"

  Yes it will. 2 goes into the top number   **6** times
  2 goes into the bottom number   **15** times

  Instead of $\frac{12}{30}$ write $\frac{6}{15}$.

- Now try again. Ask the same question. "Will 2 go into both the top number and the bottom number?"

  This time the answer is **no**. 2 will go into the top number (6), but it will not go into the bottom number, it won't go into 15 exactly.

That doesn't mean it's finished!

- Try the next **odd** number (3). "Will 3 go into both the top number and the bottom number?"

  Yes it will. 3 goes into the top number   **2** times
  3 goes into the bottom number   **5** times

  Instead of $\frac{6}{15}$ write $\frac{2}{5}$.

Up to now the the fraction $\frac{12}{30}$ has been made easier twice.

The first time the fraction became $\frac{6}{15}$ and the second time it became $\frac{2}{5}$.

Now it is finished because there are no more **odd** numbers that go into the top number and the bottom number.

You have just found out that $\frac{12}{30}$, $\frac{6}{15}$ and $\frac{2}{5}$ are all the same (equivalent fractions), but $\frac{2}{5}$ is the easiest. We say $\frac{2}{5}$ is the simplest possible form for $\frac{12}{30}$.

<u>Here is another one.</u>

$\frac{60}{300}$ of the world's population is Chinese.

- Start with 2. "Will 2 go into both the top number and the bottom number?"

    Yes it will   2 goes into the top number   **30** times.
    2 goes into the bottom number   **150** times.

    Now it is easier. $\frac{30}{150}$ of the world's population is Chinese.

- Try 2 again. "Will 2 go into both the top number and the bottom number?"

    Yes it will   2 goes into the top number   **15** times.
    2 goes into the bottom number   **75** times.

    Now it is even easier. $\frac{15}{75}$ of the world's population is Chinese.

- Try 2 again. "Will 2 go into both the top number and the bottom number?"
- No it won't, so try the next odd number. "Will 3 go into both the top number and the bottom number?"

    Yes it will   3 goes into the top number   **5** times.
    3 goes into the bottom number   **25** times.

    Even better. $\frac{5}{25}$ of the world's population is Chinese.

Try 3 again. "Will 3 go into both the top number and the bottom number?"
- No it won't, so try the next odd number. "Will 5 go into both the top number and the bottom number?"

    Yes it will.   5 goes into the top number   **1** times.
    5 goes into the bottom number   **5** times.

Wonderful. $\frac{1}{5}$ of the world's population is Chinese.

So $\frac{1}{5}$, $\frac{5}{25}$, $\frac{15}{75}$, $\frac{30}{150}$ and $\frac{60}{300}$ are all the same (equivalent fractions) but $\frac{1}{5}$ is the easiest to understand.

With practice you will be able to do it much quicker.

For example you may see that $\frac{15}{75}$ is $\frac{1}{5}$ straight away because:

        15 goes into 15   **1** time

        15 goes into 75   **5** times

Some fractions can't be made easier.

For example, $\frac{19}{53}$. There are no numbers that go into 19 **and** 53, so nothing can be done in this case.

Exercise 3

1. Simplify these fractions (make them easier).

   a). $\frac{6}{12}$ c) $\frac{3}{15}$ e) $\frac{8}{20}$ g) $\frac{12}{40}$ i) $\frac{9}{15}$

   b) $\frac{6}{8}$ d) $\frac{20}{25}$ f) $\frac{14}{35}$ h) $\frac{35}{105}$ j) $\frac{90}{360}$

   Interesting TRUE facts

2. Giant earthworms can be found in certain parts of the world and $\frac{75}{300}$ of their length is 1 metre. Make the fraction easier then work out how long giant earthworms can be.

3. Wales has a lot of beautiful scenery and $\frac{21}{126}$ of the land is National Parks. Make the fraction easier to understand.

4. $\frac{18}{150}$ of the ingredients of gunpowder is charcoal. Make the fraction easier.

5. $\frac{35}{350}$ of the speed of sound is 76 miles per hour. Make the fraction easier, then work out the speed of sound.

6. Racing pigeons can fly at great speeds. $\frac{36}{144}$ of the speed of champion pigeons is about 15 miles per hour. Make the fraction easier, then work out the speed of a champion pigeon.

7. Rich people sometimes give large sums of money to charity. $\frac{15}{90}$ of the amount that one person gave to the RSPCA was £17,000. Make the fraction easier, and then work out how much this person gave to the RSPCA.

8. $\frac{15}{105}$ of the fuel that a jumbo jet can hold in its tanks is 6,000 gallons. Make the fraction easier, then work out how much fuel a jumbo jet can hold when it is full.

Back to the Jar

This jar is 60 mm tall. It has some fluid in it.

How full would you say it is?

Carefully measure the height of fluid. It comes to 18mm.

There are 60 mm to the top of the jar so the jar is $\frac{18}{60}$ full.

This is because the jar is broken up into 60 **equal** parts (each 1mm) and the fluid reaches the 18mm mark.

But now that we have dealt with equivalent fractions we can easily see that $\frac{18}{60}$ simplifies to $\frac{3}{10}$.

Exercise 4

Each jar below is 60mm tall.

Match up the fractions below with their proper jar. The fractions are all based on approximations.

$$\frac{2}{3}, \frac{2}{5}, \frac{3}{10}, \frac{3}{4}, \frac{5}{6}, \frac{7}{10}, \frac{1}{20}, \frac{4}{15}$$

For instance, you may think jar 5 is $\frac{2}{5}$ full.

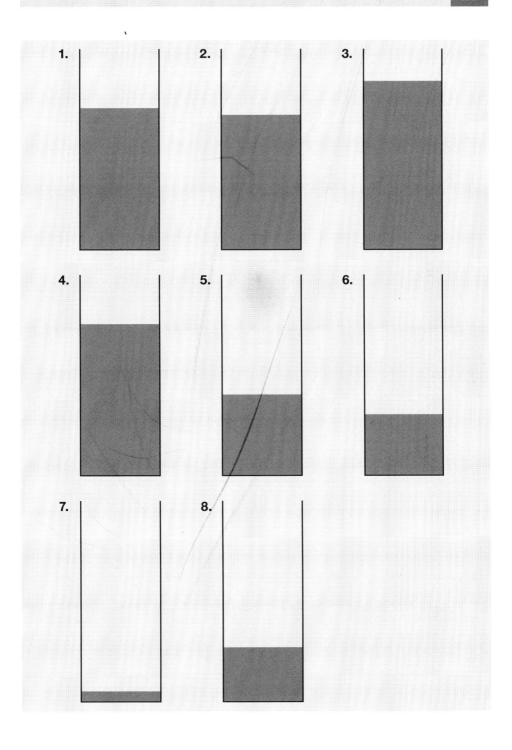

CHAPTER 2

Adding and Subtracting Fractions

2. ADDING AND SUBTRACTING FRACTIONS

Swifts (birds like swallows) stay in the air for very long periods of time without landing.

They can stay airborne for as long as $\frac{1}{3}$ of a year plus $\frac{1}{2}$ a year.

How can $\frac{1}{3}$ and $\frac{1}{2}$ be added together to see how long this is?

There are several ways of adding fractions but they can be confusing and difficult to remember. Here is a way that uses a special name to help you remember it.

This is called the **CROSSBOW METHOD.**

Follow the diagrams closely as you work through this method.

$$\frac{1}{3} \times \frac{1}{2} = \frac{+}{\quad}$$

We know the answer will be a fraction so I have drawn the line ready to receive the answer.
It is an **add** sum so I have put the **+** in.

The CROSS looks like a multiplication sign and it tells you which numbers to multiply together.

- One arm is saying 'multiply the 1 by the 2' and the other arm is saying 'multiply the 3 by the 1'.

The answer to 1 times 2 is 2. The answer to 3 times 1 is 3.

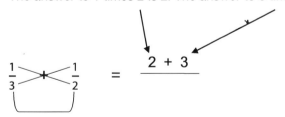

$$\frac{1}{3} \times \frac{1}{2} = \frac{2 + 3}{\quad}$$

- The BOW says 'multiply the 3 by the 2'.

The answer is 6 and it goes **underneath** the line in the answer.

$$\frac{1}{3} \times \frac{1}{2} = \frac{2 + 3}{6}$$

The **BOW** looks like a **U** (for underneath) and it is a reminder to put the answer underneath the line.

Finally, add up the numbers above the line.

$$\frac{1}{3} \times \frac{1}{2} = \frac{5}{6}$$

It's that simple! Easy wasn't it?

So $\frac{1}{3}$ of a year plus $\frac{1}{2}$ of a year is $\frac{5}{6}$ of a year. How long is that?

Remember that $\frac{5}{6}$ of a year is shorthand for "cut a year up into 6 **equal** pieces, and take 5 of the pieces."

If a year is cut up into 6 **equal** pieces then each piece will be 2 months.

Jan/Feb	Mar/Apr	May/Jun	Jul/Aug	Sep/Oct	Nov/Dec

5 of these pieces is 10 months.

Swifts can stay in the air for 10 months without landing. This may seem amazing but they have been known to stay in the air for 3 years without landing!

<u>Here is another example of adding fractions.</u>

Add $\frac{3}{10}$ of a metre and $\frac{3}{5}$ of a metre.

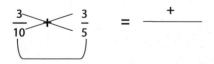

$$\frac{3}{10} \times \frac{3}{5} = \frac{+}{}$$

The first arm of the cross is saying 'multiply the 3 by the 5' (answer 15), and the second arm is saying 'multiply the 10 by the 3' (answer 30).

Put these answers above the line.

$$\frac{3}{10} \times \frac{3}{5} = \frac{15 + 30}{}$$

The BOW is saying 'multiply the 10 by the 5' (answer 50).

Remember that the BOW looks like a 'U' meaning you put it 'Underneath'.

$$\frac{3}{10} \times \frac{3}{5} = \frac{45}{50}$$

Finished again. Just as easy as the first one.

$\frac{3}{10}$ of a metre plus $\frac{3}{5}$ of a metre turns out to be $\frac{45}{50}$ of a metre.

Simplify the answer (make it easier) and work out how far this is in centimetres.

$\frac{45}{50}$ metres simplifies to $\frac{9}{10}$ metres and this is 90cm.

10cm	10cm	10cm	10cm	10cm	10cm	10cm	10cm	10cm	10cm

1 Metre

Exercise 5

1. Add these fractions using the crossbow method.

a) $\frac{1}{3} + \frac{1}{4}$ d) $\frac{1}{12} + \frac{1}{5}$ g) $\frac{1}{9} + \frac{1}{2}$

b) $\frac{1}{4} + \frac{1}{9}$ e) $\frac{1}{4} + \frac{1}{8}$ h) $\frac{1}{10} + \frac{1}{3}$

c) $\frac{1}{7} + \frac{1}{8}$ f) $\frac{1}{11} + \frac{1}{4}$

Interesting True Facts

2. Rattlesnakes are hard to kill. Even if you chop one's head off, it could still bite you $\frac{1}{6}$ of an hour plus $\frac{1}{5}$ of an hour later. How long is this?

3. The world's strongest man can lift 445 kilograms off the floor. It has been calculated that a gorilla could lift at least $\frac{1}{5}$ of a tonne plus $\frac{1}{2}$ a tonne. A tonne is 1,000 kilograms.

It is known that a bed bug has lived for $\frac{3}{14}$ of a year plus $\frac{2}{7}$ of a year.

$$\frac{3}{14} \times \frac{2}{7} = \frac{21 + 28}{98}$$

The first arm of the CROSS says 'multiply 3 by 7' and the second arm says 'multiply 14 by 2'. Put the answers on the top line.

The BOW says 'multiply 14 by 7' and put the answer underneath the line.

$$\frac{3}{14} \times \frac{2}{7} = \frac{49}{98}$$

Now we must simplify this and see how long it is.

*   Start with 2. "Will 2 go into both the top number and the bottom number?" No it won't so try the next number.

*   "Will 3 go into both the top number and the bottom number?" No it won't so try the next **odd** number.

*   "Will 5 go into both the top number and the bottom number?" No it won't so try the next **odd** number.

*   "Will 7 go into both the top number and the bottom number?" Yes it will. 7 goes into the top number 7 times, and 7 goes into the bottom number 14 times.

So the fraction simplifies to $\frac{7}{14}$. But, 7 goes into both these numbers as well.

7 goes into the top number　　**1** time
7 goes into the bottom number　**2** times

So our answer simplifies to $\frac{1}{2}$.

That means a bed bug has been known to live for $\frac{1}{2}$ a year or **6 months.**

Subtracting Fractions

Subtracting fractions is just as easy as adding them and uses the same method.

For example $\frac{1}{3} - \frac{2}{7}$.

The only difference is **we have a MINUS sign INSTEAD of a PLUS sign.**

$$\frac{1}{3} \times \frac{2}{7} = \frac{7 - 6}{21}$$

The answer is $\frac{1}{21}$.

Use the techniques you have learnt to answer the following questions.

Exercise 6

1. Add or subtract these fractions using the crossbow method.

a) $\frac{2}{7} + \frac{3}{5}$

b) $\frac{5}{8} + \frac{1}{3}$

c) $\frac{7}{9} - \frac{3}{4}$

d) $\frac{7}{8} - \frac{2}{3}$

e) $\frac{5}{8} + \frac{2}{12}$

f) $\frac{3}{2} - \frac{1}{2}$

g) $\frac{1}{2} + \frac{1}{5}$

h) $\frac{3}{8} - \frac{1}{5}$

i) $\frac{4}{5} - \frac{2}{3}$

j) $\frac{5}{12} + \frac{2}{7}$

k) $\frac{1}{2} + \frac{3}{8}$

l) $\frac{4}{7} - \frac{1}{4}$

m) $\frac{11}{12} - \frac{4}{5}$

n) $\frac{3}{7} + \frac{1}{3}$

o) $\frac{3}{4} - \frac{2}{5}$

p) $\frac{1}{4} + \frac{2}{5}$

A very good way to learn is to mark someone else's work and tell them where they went wrong.

Below is some work done by G. Hollow. Mark it. When you find a mistake, put a ring around it and say why it is wrong.

A. Hollow Exercise A

a) $\dfrac{2}{3} + \dfrac{1}{7} = \dfrac{14 + 3}{10} = \dfrac{17}{10}$ Answer

b) $\dfrac{2}{3} - \dfrac{1}{7} = \dfrac{14 + 3}{21} = \dfrac{17}{21}$ Answer

c) $\dfrac{6}{7} - \dfrac{1}{2} = \dfrac{12 - 7}{14} = \dfrac{5}{14}$ Answer

d) $\dfrac{3}{11} + \dfrac{1}{10} = \dfrac{30 + 11}{120} = \dfrac{43}{120}$ Answer

CHAPTER 3

The 24 Hour Clock

3. THE 24 HOUR CLOCK

When we want to tell the time, most of us use a system called the **'12 hour' clock**. In this system, each time occurs twice – once before midday and once after midday. For example, there are two 7 o'clocks – one in the morning and one in the evening. It is necessary to say 7am for the morning and 7pm for the evening, in order to know which time of day we are talking about.

If we use the **24 hour clock**, 7 in the morning becomes 0700 (or 07.00) and 7 in the evening becomes 1900 (or 19.00).

The 24 hour clock is used by 'clocking on' systems in factories, on timetables for ships, planes, trains and buses, and by all the armed forces, the merchant navy, and the coastguards.

How does it work?

4 digits (numbers) are used to say what the time is. The first two are for the hours and the second two are for the minutes.

The count starts at midnight (0000), which is no hours and no minutes, and then just keeps counting the hours up to 24 for the end of day.

See the chart below.

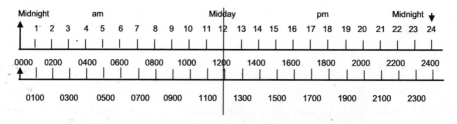

The 24 hour clock system just keeps counting from 0000 to 2400. In fact 0000 and 2400 are the same time. They are both midnight.

You may have noticed already, that when the number of hours after midnight is less than 10, a 0 is put in front so that there are always four digits. For example 0500.

This is spoken as 'oh five hundred'.

Minutes are simply attached after the hours. 1330 means 13 hours and 30 minutes (after midnight), or half past one in the afternoon.

0825 is twenty five minutes past eight in the morning (8.25am).

1720 is twenty past five in the afternoon (5.20pm).

1940 is forty minutes past seven in the evening. You would probably say 'twenty to eight'.

You can see that, like fractions, the 24 hour clock is another type of mathematical short-hand.

Exercise 7

1. Change the following times to 24 hour clock time.

    a) Ten past 8 in the morning.
    b) Ten past 8 in the evening.
    c) Quarter to 3 in the afternoon.
    d) Quarter to 3 in the morning.
    e) Twenty past 10 in the evening.
    f) Ten to 11 in the morning.
    g) Five to 11 in the morning.
    h) Five to midnight.

2. Change these time back to 12 hour clock times.

    a) 1430   c) 0745   e) 1920   g) 1640
    b) 2135   d) 0001   f) 0518   h) 1750

Part of a seaman's job in the navy is to 'keep watch'. This means standing at one of the lookout points and keeping an eye out for other ships, or land, or icebergs, or submarine periscopes if it is war time.

Each watch is normally 4 hours long and they go on all day and all night. Seamen have to take it in turns to do these watches **as well as** all their normal duties.

Dog watches

The favourite watches are the dog watches because they are only 2 hours long.

Exercise 8

1. The first 'dog watch' is from 1600 to 1800.
    What time is this using the 12 hour clock?

2. The second 'dog watch' is for the next two hours.
    When is this in 24 hour clock time?

3. The 'middle watch' is from midnight to 4 in the morning.
    When is this in the 24 hour clock time?

Eight bells

You have probably all heard the words 'eight bells'. This is a naval term. During a 'watch' a bell is sounded every half hour. It rings once for every half an hour that has passed. The 'morning watch' starts at 0400 and finishes at 0800. The bell will be rung once at 0430 (because one half hour has gone by) and then twice at 0500 (because two half hours have gone by). After 4 hours it will be rung 8 times because 8 half hours have gone by. So 8 bells means the end of the watch. Another seaman now takes over and the bells will start again with one ring after the first half hour.

4. The 'first watch' starts at 8 in the evening. What is the time when 5 bells are rung? Give the answer in 24 hour clock time.

5. Here is a story being told by a seaman to a landlubber (someone who does not go to sea). Change all the times in the story to the 12 hour clock time so that the landlubber can understand when the events of the story took place. Remember that the 'middle watch' starts at midnight.

    'I was on the 'middle watch' when it happened – 10 minutes after 3 bells to be exact. This thing surfaced and followed us for 30 minutes. Then it started leaping in and out of the water. 5 minutes before the next bell it dived out of sight and didn't come back.'

6. The 'afternoon watch' starts at midday and ends at 4pm.
    How many bells will be rung at 1530?

7. In the armed forces you often have to get back to the barracks by 2359.

What time is this using the 12 hour clock?

8. In order to catch the tide, a boat sails at twenty to nine in the morning. When is this in 24 hour clock time?

9. An SOS was sent at 1735. What time was this using the 12 hour clock?

10. If 7 minutes is added to 1855 the answer is NOT 1862. What IS the answer?

CHAPTER 4

Multiplying and Dividing Fractions

4. MULTIPLYING AND DIVIDING FRACTIONS

Multiplying Fractions

Before you can successfully multiply and divide fractions, you must understand two very important points. The first is that a whole number can be turned into a fraction just by putting a 1 underneath it.

This means that 6 and $\frac{6}{1}$ are the same thing. Think about $\frac{6}{1}$ cameras. This is shorthand for "cut a camera up into 1 **equal** piece, and take 6 of the pieces". If something is cut up into 1 piece, then it isn't cut up at all – it is left whole. Therefore when you take 6 of the pieces, you are taking 6 whole cameras.

So you can see it makes sense to say that $\frac{6}{1}$ just means 6 whole ones.

That is the first thing done. $\frac{6}{1}$ is the same as 6.

$\frac{14}{1}$ is the same as 14

$\frac{352}{1}$ is the same as 352

ANY WHOLE number can be written as a fraction by putting a 1 underneath it.

The second point you must understand is that 'OF' means 'TIMES'. This is always true in mathematics

$\frac{1}{2}$ of 8 (you know the answer is 4) means $\frac{1}{2}$ **times** 8 and the answer could be worked out by doing a multiplication.

Once again there is a special name to help you to remember how to multiply fractions. It is called the **ARROW METHOD**. Here's how it works.

To multiply $\frac{2}{3}$ by $\frac{3}{4}$, you need to write out the sum.

$\frac{2}{3} \times \frac{3}{4} =$ ———   and put the line ready for the answer.

Now put the **arrows** in.

$$\frac{2}{3} \times \frac{3}{4} = \text{———}$$

Now multiply the numbers that the arrows touch; and put the answers above and underneath the answer line.

$$\frac{2}{3} \times \frac{3}{4} = \frac{6}{12}$$

And that's the answer. EASY isn't it?

Yes, it could be simplified to $\frac{1}{2}$, but the actual fraction multiplication has been done!

Example

A nurse with Captain's rank is paid about $\frac{3}{5}$ of £2,915 per week.

Remember 'OF' means 'TIMES'. $\frac{3}{5}$ of 2,915 means $\frac{3}{5}$ times 2,915.

Write the problem out as a multiplying fraction sum.

$$\frac{3}{5} \times \frac{2,915}{1} = \frac{8,745}{5}$$ (2,915 was turned into a fraction by putting a 1 underneath it.)

Now that the multiplication is done, perhaps it can be simplified.

*   Start with 2. "Will 2 go into both the top number and the bottom number?"

*   No it won't, so try 3. "Will 3 go both into the top number and the bottom number?"

*   No it won't, so try 5. "Will 5 go both into the top number and the bottom number?"

Yes it will.   5 goes into the top number   **1,749** times
                      5 goes into the bottom number   **1** times

So the answer simplifies to $\frac{1,749}{1}$ **but** this is just 1749.

Final answer. The Captain's pay is about £1,749 per week.

Exercise 9

1. Multiply these fractions using the ARROW method.

    a) $\frac{5}{9}$ x $\frac{3}{4}$ c) $\frac{2}{3}$ x $\frac{4}{5}$ e) $\frac{2}{5}$ x $\frac{3}{7}$

    b) $\frac{3}{8}$ x $\frac{1}{2}$ d) $\frac{6}{7}$ x $\frac{2}{3}$ f) $\frac{7}{8}$ x $\frac{5}{7}$

2. In the next questions, remember that 'of' means 'times' and that a whole number can be turned into a fraction by putting a 1 underneath it.

    a) What is $\frac{3}{7}$ of 63?

    b) What is $\frac{8}{12}$ of 60?

    c) What is $\frac{7}{8}$ of 56?

    d) What is $\frac{2}{3}$ of 120?

    e) What is $\frac{3}{4}$ of 88?

    f) What is $\frac{4}{5}$ of 90?

Interesting True Facts.

3. The number of bones in the human body is $\frac{2}{5}$ of 515. How many is that?

4. An oyster has been known to live for $\frac{5}{9}$ of 144 years. How long is that?

5. The Death Cap is a poisonous toadstool. $\frac{5}{7}$ of 42 grams of it is enough to kill someone. How many grams is this?

6. One day on the planet Mercury is much longer than a day on Earth. One Mercury day is $\frac{1}{5}$ of 295 Earth days. How many Earth days is this?

At this stage, we would like to make a point...

You have been doing a lot of work with numbers and, in some cases, there are quicker ways of doing things. We have left these out on purpose because if you try to do too much all in one go, it just becomes confusing. Confusion is bad; it will make you lose interest. But don't worry, more advanced techniques will be learnt in time.

Dividing Fractions

Mathematicians use a clever method to divide fractions. They found that if they turned the **last** fraction upside down **and changed the 'divide' to a 'multiply'**, they got the right answer.

It may seem silly, but **it works**, and is **easy!**

$$\frac{2}{3} \div \frac{4}{5} = \underline{\qquad}$$

$$\frac{2}{3} \times \frac{5}{4} = \underline{\qquad} \qquad\qquad \textbf{Last fraction turned upside down and } \div \textbf{ changed to x}$$

Now multiply.

$$\frac{2}{3} \times \frac{5}{4} = \frac{10}{12} \qquad\qquad \text{DONE. That is the answer...but it simplifies to } \frac{5}{6}.$$

Easy. $\frac{5}{6}$ is the answer to the original divide sum.

Exercise 10

1. Solve these division sums. Question E may trick you; but just remember these are fraction sums.

   a) $\frac{1}{2} \div \frac{3}{4}$ b) $\frac{5}{8} \div \frac{7}{9}$ c) $\frac{2}{3} \div \frac{4}{5}$

   d) $\frac{1}{9} \div \frac{3}{1}$ e) $\frac{3}{5} \div 4$ f) $\frac{3}{11} \div \frac{1}{2}$

   g) $\frac{5}{7} \div \frac{3}{4}$ h) $\frac{7}{8} \div \frac{2}{9}$ i) $\frac{6}{15} \div \frac{3}{4}$

   j) $\frac{7}{12} \div \frac{5}{6}$

Dividing Fractions

If the number on the top of a fraction is bigger than the number on the bottom of the fraction, then the fraction is bigger than 1 whole one.

For example $\frac{11}{2}$. This means "cut something up into 2 **equal** pieces, and take 11 of the pieces."

Every time you take 2 pieces you have got a whole one, because things were cut up into 2 equal pieces.

1   2   3   4   5

11 pieces is enough to make 5 whole ones with one piece left over.

What this amounts to is 'How many times does 2 go into 11?'

(How many times does the bottom number go into the top number?)

The answer is 5 with one left over.

So $\frac{11}{2}$ equals $5\frac{1}{2}$. (That is 5 whole ones and one piece left over)

What about $\frac{17}{3}$? In this case, we cut something up into 3 equal pieces.

Therefore it takes 3 pieces to make up a whole one. We have 17 pieces and every time we take 3 of them that will be one whole one.

How many lots of 3 can we get out of 17?

||| ||| ||| ||| ||| ||

1   2   3   4   5

The answer is **5** whole ones with **2** pieces left over.

What this amounts to is 'How many times does 3 go into 17'

So $\frac{17}{3}$ equals $5\frac{2}{3}$.

Answer: **5** times remainder **2**. Which gives the same answer

It was just a case of seeing how many groups of 3 could be made out of 17 pieces (each group of 3 is 1 whole one). You could do it by dividing 3 into 17 (that would be the mathematician's way of doing it). Writing it out in full for example, $\frac{45}{7}$, would be a bit difficult.

| | | | | | | | | | | | | | | | | | | | | | | | | | | | | | | | | | | | | | | | | | | | |

   1   2   3   4   5   6

$$\frac{45}{7} = 6\frac{3}{7}$$

The mathematician's way. How may 7s can we get out of 45 pieces?

7 into 45 goes **6** remainder **3** so this is a quick way of getting the answer.

This shows how important it is to know your timetables. If you make the effort to master them, you will find things become easier as the work progresses.

Fractions should always be made easier (simplified) if possible.

For example $\frac{26}{6}$. The top number is bigger than the bottom number so the fraction is bigger than 1 whole one, but the fraction can be simplified first.

2 goes into the top number   **13** times
2 goes into the bottom number   **3** times

Therefore $\frac{26}{6}$ is the same as $\frac{13}{3}$

There are 13 pieces in the fraction and it takes 3 pieces to make 1 whole one.

$13 \div 3 = 4$ with 1 piece left over.

We can get 4 whole ones out of 13 (this will use 12 pieces) and there will be 1 piece left over.

Answer $\frac{26}{6} = 4\frac{1}{3}$

Simplifying the fraction first made the whole job easier.

Try it yourself with $\frac{94}{10}$. The answer is $9\frac{2}{5}$ but do it yourself to make sure.

Things to remember

* Always make a fraction easier (simplify it) if it is possible to do so.

* If the final answer has a bigger number on the top than on the bottom, then the fraction is bigger than 1 whole number. Change it back into whole ones and fractions.

Exercise 11

1. Change the following to whole numbers and fractions.

a) $\frac{28}{8}$ c) $\frac{14}{3}$ e) $\frac{34}{5}$ g) $\frac{54}{7}$ i) $\frac{91}{4}$

b) $\frac{45}{2}$ d) $\frac{48}{3}$ f) $\frac{17}{3}$ h) $\frac{26}{4}$ j) $\frac{31}{6}$

Adding Fractions with Whole Numbers

In order to deal with sums like $2\frac{1}{2} + 3\frac{2}{3}$ it is necessary to change everything into fractions first, and then continue as normal.

To change $2\frac{1}{2}$ into a fraction:
Each whole one is cut up into 2 equal pieces.
First whole one   second whole one   the extra half

| | | | |

That makes a total of 5 pieces and each piece is a half.
Therefore $2\frac{1}{2} = \frac{5}{2}$ (5 halves)

To change $3\frac{2}{3}$ into a fraction:

Each whole one is cut up into 3 equal pieces.

First one   second one   third one   extra thirds

| | | | | | | | | | | **(a total of 11 thirds)**

$3\frac{2}{3} = \frac{11}{3}$

Now the original problem can be done.

$2\frac{1}{2} + 3\frac{2}{3} = \frac{5}{2} + \frac{11}{3}$

$\frac{5}{2} + \frac{11}{3} = \frac{15 + 22}{6} = \frac{37}{6}$

Final answer $6\frac{1}{6}$

Quick method for changing whole number and fractions into all fractions.

$2\frac{1}{2}$

Multiply these two and add the top one, 2 x 2 is 4 plus 1 is 5. (a total of 5 halves).

$$2\frac{1}{2} = \frac{5}{2}$$

$3\frac{2}{3}$

Multiply these two and add the top one, 3 x 3 is 9 plus 2 is 11. (a total of 11 thirds).

$$3\frac{2}{3} = \frac{11}{3}$$

The above method for breaking whole numbers and fractions into all fractions is just a mathematical way of doing it instead of writing everything down and then adding it all up. It is obviously more professional to do it this way but the diagram method was just to explain it.

Things to remember

In all fraction problems, the routine is the same:

*   First, break all the whole numbers up into fractions;
*   Second, do the fraction problem in the normal way;
*   Third, simplify and change the answer back to whole numbers if possible.

Multiplying or Dividing Fractions with Whole Numbers

Once again we need to break the numbers up into fractions.

Let's work through an example: $2\frac{3}{5}$ x $1\frac{5}{7}$.

Break $2\frac{3}{5}$ up into fractions.

We will do it the professional way.

$2\frac{3}{5}$

Multiply 2 by 5 and add the 3. 2 times 5 equals 10, plus 3 equals 13.

$$2\frac{3}{5} = \frac{13}{5}$$

Similarly for $1\frac{5}{7}$.

$1\frac{5}{7}$

Multiply 1 by 7 and add the 5. 1 times 7 equals 7, plus 5 equals 12.

$$1\frac{5}{7} = \frac{12}{7}$$

Now just do the sum in the normal way.

$$2\frac{3}{5} \times 1\frac{5}{7} = \frac{13}{5} \times \frac{12}{7} = \frac{156}{35}$$

Change the answer back to whole numbers and fractions.
It takes 35 pieces to make 1 whole one so how many 35's can we get out of 156 pieces?

35	70	105	140
1 lot of 35	2 lots of 35	3 lots of 35	4 lots of 35

4 lots of 35 come to 140 so there are 4 whole ones and 16 left over.

Final answer $2\frac{3}{5} \times 1\frac{5}{7} = 4\frac{16}{35}$

Suppose it had been a divide sum.

$$2\frac{3}{5} \div 1\frac{5}{7}$$

Turn it into all fractions. (We have already done that above)

$$2\frac{3}{5} \div 1\frac{5}{7} = \frac{13}{5} \div \frac{12}{7} = \frac{13}{5} \times \frac{7}{12} = \frac{91}{60}$$

Turn the last fraction upside down and change the ÷ to x.

Final answer $\frac{91}{60}$ or $1\frac{31}{60}$

Exercise 12

1. Find the answers to the following questions. Remember to break the whole numbers up into fractions before you start.

   a) $2\frac{1}{2} \times 3\frac{1}{2}$ c) $2\frac{7}{8} - 2\frac{3}{5}$

   b) $3\frac{5}{8} \div 1\frac{2}{3}$ d) $1\frac{5}{6} + 1\frac{1}{2}$

Interesting True Facts

2. Jumbo jets use a lot of fuel. Instead of being calculated as miles per gallon, their fuel consumption is calculated in **gallons per mile.** The number of gallons per mile can be found by working out $2\frac{1}{2} \div \frac{2}{7}$.

3. Humming birds are the world's smallest birds. It takes a lot of them to weigh just one ounce. The number needed to weigh 1 ounce is $\frac{2}{3} \div \frac{1}{27}$.

4. How many million dogs do you think there are in Britain?

   The answer is $1\frac{1}{4} \times 4\frac{2}{5}$.

5. Solar panels can be fitted onto the roof of a house. They pick up the heat from the sun (even when the sun is not shining) and use it to heat water for the house. How much of the electricity bill do you think they save?

   The answer is $\frac{3}{5} + \frac{1}{15}$.

6. 6 metres up a rope is a long way. It would probably take you about 30 seconds to climb it.

   The world's record (in seconds) for climbing it using **hands only** is $3\frac{2}{3} - 1\frac{4}{15}$.

CHAPTER 5

Brain Teasers

5. BRAIN TEASERS

Mathematicians have proved it is possible to get to the centre of any maze by following a simple rule. The **secret of the maze.**

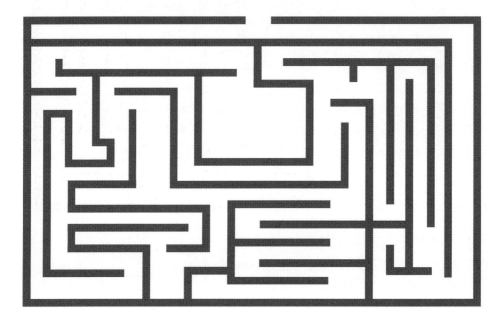

Enter the maze and put your hand on one of the walls. It doesn't matter which one. You can touch either the left wall or the right wall. Now just keep walking without taking your hand off the wall. In other words, just keep following the wall you are touching.

You will always end up in the middle of the maze. It won't be the **quickest** way to get there, but it always works. You can get back out by doing the same thing – just follow a wall.

Which gets you to the centre quickest?

> **1.** Entering the maze, turning left and keeping your left hand on the left wall.
> **2.** Entering the maze, turning right and keeping your right hand on the right wall.

Now you know the secret of mazes. But it is still possible to fool you!

Try the method on the maze below and see what strange thing happens. Can you explain it?

Answer on Page 51.

Taking Away Without Taking Away

This sounds odd, doesn't it? It can be done though.
426 - 58 can be solved by adding.

<u>Here is how:</u>
Start by making both numbers the same length. This can be done by putting a 0 in front of the shorter one.

426 – 58 becomes 426 – 058.

```
 426
- 058
```

Now make the 3 digits on the bottom up to 9 by **adding** the necessary amount:

Add **9** to 0 to make it 9
Add **4** to 5 to make it 9
Add **1** to 8 to make it 9

Change the bottom numbers in the sum to these 3 new numbers. (9, 4 and 1)

Now the sum is
```
 426
- 941
```

Now change the – to +

Now the sum is
```
 426
+941
```

Now add them up

```
 426
+941
1367
```

Finally, chop off the left hand digit to get 367, and add an extra 1 to it to get 368.

426 – 58 = 368 and this is the correct answer.

We worked it out by adding and it works every time.

Computers sometimes use this method because then they don't need to have extra equipment to do subtractions.

Let's work through another example. 4,893 – 2,976.
Both numbers are the same length so we don't have to add any 0s to make them the same length.

In order to make 2,976 into 9,999 we need **7,023** because the 2 needs **7** to make it up to 9. The 9 needs **0** to make it up to 9 (it already **is** 9). The 7 needs **2** to make it up to 9; and the 6 needs **3** to make it up to 9.

Now rewrite the sum and change the – to +.

```
 4893
+7023
```

Add it up.

```
 4,893
+7,023
11,916
```

Chop the left hand number off, and add 1 to the answer (1,916 + 1).

Answer 1,917

Exercise 13

Subtract these numbers using the adding technique.

1. 473 − 85
2. 111 − 49
3. 746 − 573
4. 204 − 76
5. 3004 − 745

6. 7510 − 2486
7. 20567 − 783
8. 693573 − 48686
9. 4782735421 − 378958676
10. 2765337465234 − 276457863542

Do not get confused by the big numbers! Treat them exactly the same way.

The only thing to be careful about is keeping the digits exactly underneath each other starting at the **right hand end.**

For example:

```
 2765337465234
-0276457863542
```

Now you can change all the numbers on the bottom line as we did in the examples above and change the sign to a +.

Keeping the numbers (digits) exactly underneath each other is **extremely** important and will be needed a lot in this book.

Mathematics teaches you to be tidy and this is something employers like.
If you are untidy, you will probably get the wrong answer.

Answer to the maze.
What happened was that you went into the maze, followed the wall and eventually came out of the maze without ever getting to the centre.

This is because the drawing is 2 mazes. There is another small maze inside the centre of the first maze – so you get to the centre of the first maze and then come out again without ever getting into the second maze.

The method works for **any single** maze – but not when a second maze is inside the first one!

This is the second maze
inside the first one.

CHAPTER 6

Multiplication of Whole Numbers

6. MULTIPLICATION OF WHOLE NUMBERS

In spite of the fact that most people today use calculators, there are still a lot of jobs where you may need to do some arithmetic without one.

The ability to do basic calculations quickly and accurately will always be useful – there are lots of things you might miss out on if you can't – including getting a job. Do yourself a favour and learn all the arithmetic you can.

Nearly everybody makes the same mistake with long multiplication. They manage the multiplication correctly but they get the answers in the wrong column.
Here is a way of doing it that helps you get the answers in the correct column.

EXAMPLE

251 x 47

To find the starting place when multiplying by 7.
Draw an arrow down through the first column.
Draw another arrow where the answer will go.
Where the arrows cross is the **starting** place.
The answer starts at the starting place.

Multiply the top line by 7.

```
  251
   47
 1757
```

NOTE that the answer starts in the starting place and then moves left.

To multiply by 4, we need to find the new starting place.

To find the starting place when multiplying by 4.
Draw an arrow down through the **second** column.
Draw another arrow where the answer will go.
Where the arrows cross is the **starting** place.
The answer starts at the starting place.

Now multiply the top line by 4, and put the first answer in the **starting place**.

```
   251
    47
  1757
 1004
```

NOTE that the answer starts in the starting place (under the 5) and then moves left.

Now just add up the two rows in the answer to get the final answer.

```
   251
    47
 1757
 1004
11797
```
          This is the correct answer.

It is **easy** if you are careful and use the method above to find the starting place, (where you put the first number in each row of the answer).

Let's do a slightly longer one.

682 x 295

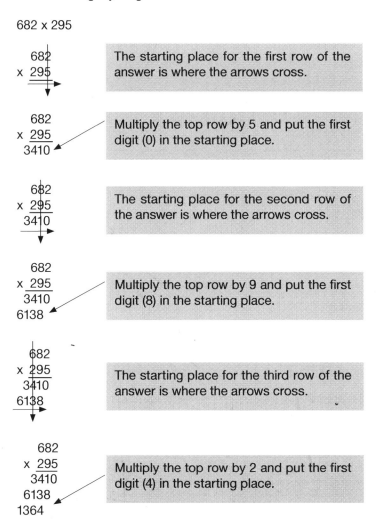

```
  682
x 295
```
The starting place for the first row of the answer is where the arrows cross.

```
  682
x 295
 3410
```
Multiply the top row by 5 and put the first digit (0) in the starting place.

```
  682
x 295
 3410
```
The starting place for the second row of the answer is where the arrows cross.

```
  682
x 295
 3410
 6138
```
Multiply the top row by 9 and put the first digit (8) in the starting place.

```
  682
x 295
 3410
 6138
```
The starting place for the third row of the answer is where the arrows cross.

```
  682
x 295
 3410
 6138
 1364
```
Multiply the top row by 2 and put the first digit (4) in the starting place.

Now everything has been kept neatly in the right place and all we have to do is add up the 3 rows of the answer.

```
     682
  x  295
    3410
    6138
    1364
  201190
```

NOTE how the numbers are all kept perfectly in line underneath each other.
It is only by being so neat and tidy that we know which numbers to add together at the end.

Answer 201,190

Exercise 14

1. Find the answers to the following sums. When you have done them, check your answers and make sure you understand how multiplication works before you go on to the next questions.

   a) 27 x 14   e) 48 x 23   i) 74 x 35

   b) 68 x 19   f) 134 x 22   j) 628 x 12

   c) 412 x 26   g) 632 x 123   k) 517 x 351

   d) 486 x 987   h) 1234 x 756   l) 36872 x 532

Interesting True Facts

2. Roughly 507 x 69 people die of snake bites each year. How many is this?

3. A flea can jump 130 times its own height. If a 6 foot person jumped 130 times their own height, how high would this be?

4. A jumbo jet can hold 1985 x 21 gallons of fuel. How many gallons is this?

5. The number of cats in Britain is roughly 111111 x 45. How many is this?

6. The largest piece of gold ever found was 110 x 32 ounces. How many ounces is this?

7. Using your answer to Q6, how much is the largest piece of gold worth? Gold is £230 an ounce.

8. The ancient Mayan Indians of Central America had some unusual names for counting days.

   1 TUN = 360 days

   1 KATUN = 20 TUNS

   1 BAKTUN = 20 KATUNS

How many days are there in a KATUN? (20 lots of 360)

How many days are there in a BAKTUN?

9. The Mayan Indians also had things called 'long counts'. 1.5.3 is a long count.

   It means 1 BAKTUN plus 5 KATUNS plus 3 TUNS.

   How many days are there in the long count 1.5.3?

10. There is an old Chinese tale which tells the story of an Emperor who became bored and asked his mathematician to invent a new game for him. The mathematician was a very clever man and he invented the game of chess.

    The Emperor was delighted and told the inventor he could have any reward he wanted.

    The mathematician said, 'Pay me by putting 1 grain of rice on the first square of the chessboard, 2 grains on the second square, 4 grains on the third square, 8 grains on the fourth square, 16 grains on the fifth square' and so on.

    The Emperor thought this was very reasonable; **until he came to do it!**

    There are 64 squares on the chess board.

    When the Emperor found he couldn't do it, he is said to have become very cross and ordered the mathematician to be beheaded!

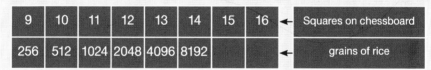

9	10	11	12	13	14	15	16	← Squares on chessboard
256	512	1024	2048	4096	8192			← grains of rice

The first 14 squares of the chess board have been worked out.

How many pieces of rice would be on square 20?

How many would be on square 40?

You just have to keep doubling the number every time – but it gets very large and it is difficult to get it right.

In fact there wouldn't be enough rice in the whole world to cover square 64.

11. The chance of winning the football pools is very low.

    There is only 1 chance in 55930 x 18603

    Do the multiplication to find out what the chance is.

CHAPTER 7

Bar charts and Pie Charts

7. BAR CHARTS AND PIE CHARTS

This is all about collecting data and facts and displaying it in ways that are easily understood.
A sheet full of numbers is of no use at all until the numbers have been displayed in a meaningful manner – usually some form of chart from which it is easy to read and compare them.

Bar Charts and Frequency Tables
Here are some facts about the highest mountains in different countries.

COUNTRY	HIGHEST MOUNTAIN	HEIGHT IN METRES
Italy	Mt Viso	3841
W Germany	Zugspitze	2962
Switzerland	Finsteraarhorn	4274
Scotland	Ben Nevis	1345
Morocco	Dj. Ighil	4167
England	Scafell Pike	978
France	Mt. Blanc	4810
Austria	Glockner	3798
Spain	Mt. Perdido	3355
Wales	Snowdon	1085
Sweden	Kebnekaise	2106

A **Bar Chart** will show these facts more clearly.

First draw a pair of axes (two straight lines at right angles to each other).
Put the height in metres up the left hand side as shown in the diagram.

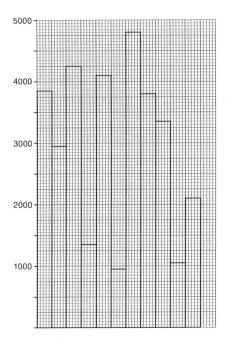

But there is more to it than just that.

It is important that bar charts are drawn accurately. Sometimes it helps to draw them larger to make it easier to plot where the bars should reach. The spaces between the numbers on the left should be worked out carefully.

This is called getting the **scale** right.

The next diagram is much better. The whole page has been used and it is a lot easier to read. The height of the bars can be worked out more accurately, because there are more numbers on the scale (left of the chart).

Also the bars have been drawn across the whole width of the page and this makes it easier to put labels on it.

Everything is nicely labelled. The chart uses the whole page. There is a **title**.

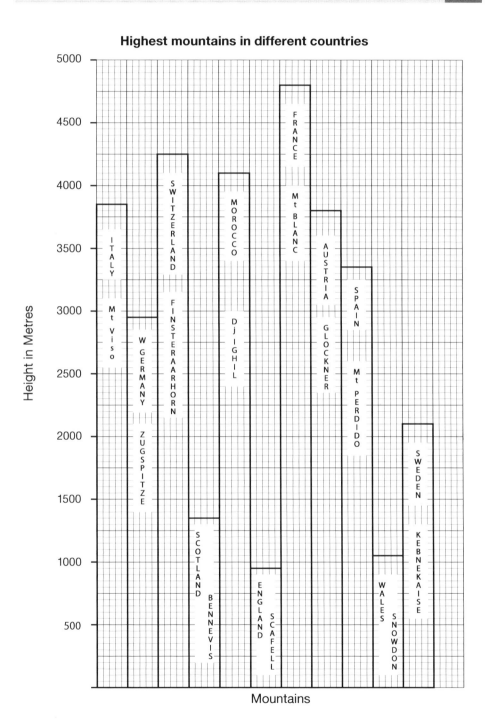

Highest mountains in different countries

Exercise 15

Draw bar charts to show the following information.

1. Number of days which are public holidays.

Austria	13 days
Belgium	10 days
Luxembourg	13 days
Czechoslovakia	6 days
Denmark	13 days
Britain	8 days
Italy	16 days
Finland	13 days
France	15 days
Switzerland	9 days
W. Germany	19 days
Spain	19 days

2. Motorway speed limits

Belgium	74 mph
Netherlands	62 mph
Luxembourg	75 mph
Spain	80 mph
France	86 mph
Britain	70 mph
W. Germany	80 mph
Portugal	62 mph

The next exercise uses bar charts to see if different pieces of writing were written by the same person.

Paragraph 1

A tramp, and a hard looking one, said Ben to himself.
He hesitated about answering, being naturally reluctant to have such a traveling companion.
"Well, what do you say?" demanded the tramp rather impatiently.
"There's plenty of room on that seat, and I'm dead tired."
"Where are you going?"
"Same way you are, to Pentonville."
"You can ride," said Ben.

Paragraph 2

First he went to the barn and filled one pocket
you see, he was a big boy now and had pockets
one, two, three, four, five, six, seven
one over his heart, two close by his belt, one on the inside of his jacket
one on each side of his hips and two in the back of his corduroy trousers.

Paragraph 3

Dick led the way, and the gentleman followed him into the store.
At the reappearance of Dick in such company, the clerk flushed a little, and looked nervous.
He fancied that he could browbeat a youngster, but with a gentleman he saw that it would be a different matter. He turned around and began replacing some goods on the shelves.

The way to do it is to take one paragraph at a time and count how many words have just one letter, how many words have just two letters, and so on.

Start with paragraph 1. There are 3 words with 1 letter, there are 8 words with 2 letters and there are 15 words with 3 letters. But there is a better way of writing this down.

Something called a **frequency** table is used. Frequency is a word that means **'how often something happens'**.
In paragraph 1, the frequency of 2 letter words is 8. In other words 2 letter words happen 8 times.

Frequency table for paragraph 1

Word length	1	2	3	4	5	6	7	8	9	10	11	12
Frequency	3	8	15	15	5	3	2	1	5	0	2	0

Check that the table is correct. Are there 13 words with 4 letters and 3 words with 6 letters? Check it all, and, when you are happy with it draw a bar chart.

Bar Chart for Paragraph 1

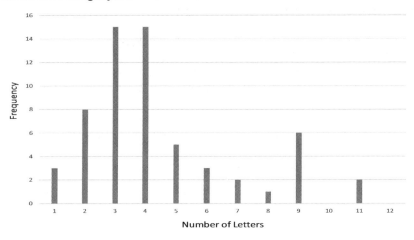

Now do the same thing for the other two paragraphs.
It will be possible to see which two were written by the same person because two of the bar charts will have almost the same shape but the other one will be different.

Pie Charts

Another way of putting information into a diagram is a **Pie Chart**.
It is called a pie chart because it is shaped like a round pie and you cut it up into slices.

The only problem is deciding how big the slices should be.

A Nobel prize is given every year to people who have done the best work in certain subjects.

Here is a list of countries to which some of the past prize winners for **medicine** have belonged.

Germany	10 winners
Netherlands	3 winners
Austria	5 winners
Denmark	4 winners
Sweden	4 winners

| Italy | 2 winners |
| Britain | 17 winners |

First, count how many things have to go onto the chart altogether. In this case the 'things' are the Nobel prize winners for medicine.

If you add together all the prize winners you will find there are 45 of them.
(17 + 2 + 4 + 4 + 5 + 3 + 10)
Each winner must get their fair share of the pie.
The pie is a circle and a circle has 360 degrees in it, so we have to divide 360 into 45 equal slices.

Use a calculator, if you like, to work out 360 ÷ 45. Answer 360 ÷ 45 = 8

So each winner will get 8 degrees of the circle.

Now make a list of how big each country's slice will be.

Germany has 10 winners. Each winner gets 8 degrees.
Germany will have 80 degrees (10 x 8).

The Netherlands has 3 winners. Each winner gets 8 degrees.
The Netherlands will have 24 degrees (3 x 8).

Write this out as another list.

Germany	80 degrees (10 x 8)
Netherlands	24 degrees (3 x 8)
Austria	40 degrees (5 x 8)
Denmark	32 degrees (4 x 8)
Sweden	32 degrees (4 x 8)
Italy	16 degrees (2 x 8)
Britain	136 degrees (17 x 8)

That's the main bit of arithmetic done.

Now draw a circle and put a line from the centre up to the top.

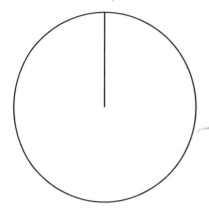

Place the protractor as shown and make a mark at the 80° (for Germany).

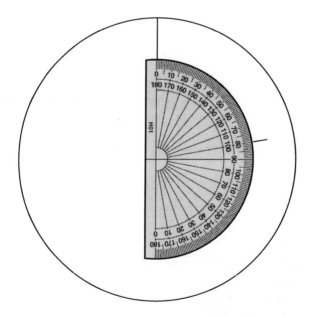

Remove the protractor and draw a line from the centre passing through the 80° mark you made. That is the German slice drawn.

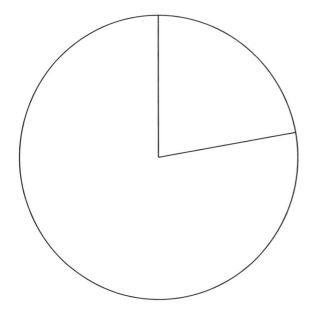

Now place the protractor as shown and make a mark at 24° (for the Netherlands slice).

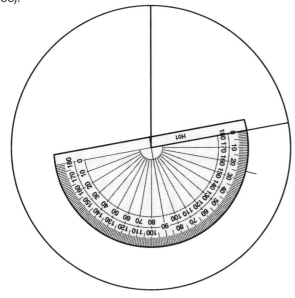

Remove the protractor and draw a line from the centre passing through the 24° mark you made. That is the Netherlands slice drawn.

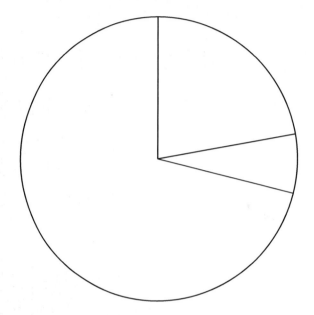

Continue slicing up the pie until all the slices are done.

Pie Chart showing Nobel Prize winners for Medicine

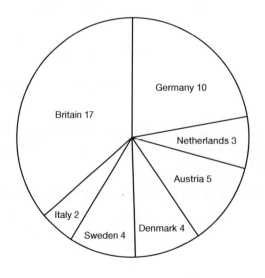

Germany 10

Britain 17

Netherlands 3

Austria 5

Italy 2

Sweden 4

Denmark 4

Each slice has been labelled to make it easy to understand.

Exercise 16

Draw up a pie chart for each of the following.

1. Here is a list showing the number of eggs you might expect to find in the nests of different birds.

Golden Eagle	2 eggs
Robin	6 eggs
Blue Tit	12 eggs
Swan	4 eggs
Partridge	16 eggs

2. Here is a list of money spent by firms on TV advertising.

Things advertised	Amount spent in £ million per year
Packet soups	37
Pickles	25
Salad dressings	24
Instant milk / creamers	36
Instant / canned potatoes	13
Bleaches & lavatory cleaners	45

A survey involves collecting information in order to find something out.

For example, asking people which toothpaste they use in order to find out which is the most popular.

A **car survey** is interesting. You would be able to find out which one came from farthest away. It is possible to tell where a car was registered by looking at its number plate. Count British cars only.

The first thing to do though is carry out the survey and for this a **tally sheet** is

```
┌─────────────────────────────────────────────────────┐
│                    TALLY SHEET                        │
│                     Car Survey                        │
│                                                       │
│   SURVEY carried out by.............................  │
│                                                       │
│   Date...................Place......................  │
│                                                       │
├─────────────────────────────────────────────────────┤
│  TALLY                                                │
│                                                       │
│                                                       │
│                                                       │
├─────────────────────────────────────────────────────┤
│  Registration numbers                                 │
│                                                       │
│                                                       │
│                                                       │
│                                                       │
│                                                       │
│                                                       │
│                                                       │
└─────────────────────────────────────────────────────┘
```

Tally is just another word for '**count**'. The normal way of keeping tally (keeping count) is to put a stroke every time you count something, and then cross them out again when the count reaches 5. Then do the same thing again.

After you take12 car numbers your tally would like this ~~||||~~ ~~||||~~ ||

The reason for doing it this way is that it is easy to count up in batches of 5.
You can easily keep track of how many registration numbers you have collected.

It is a good idea to collect a number that makes it easy to draw a pie chart.
45, 60 72 and 90 are good numbers.

Finding out where the cars came from.

Below is a complete list of registration offices for cars registered from 2001 to 2014. Suppose the number was **GL 53 AHC**. Take the first letter **(G)** and look it up in the supplied list. You will find that the car comes from Maidstone or Brighton. Look at the second letter **(L)** and it belongs to Maidstone.

| (G) | **Maidstone** | A B C D E F G H J K L M N O |
| | **Brighton** | P R S T U V W X Y |

First letter	Place	Second letter
	Peterborough	A B C D E F G H J K L M N
A	Norwich	O P R S T U
	Ipswich	V W X Y
B	Birmingham	A–Y
	Cardiff	A B C D E F G H J K L M N O
C	Swansea	P R S T U V
	Bangor	W X Y
D	Chester	A B C D E F G H J K
	Shrewsbury	L M N O P R S T U V W X Y
E	Chelmsford	A–Y
F	Nottingham	A B C D E F G H J K L M N P
	Lincoln	R S T V W X Y
G	Maidstone	A B C D E F G H J K L M N O
	Brighton	P R S T U V W X Y
	Bournemouth	A B C D E F G H J
H	Portsmouth	K L M N O P R S T U V W X Y Note: HW for **Isle of Wight** residents only
K	Northampton	A B C D E F G H J K L M N O P R S T U V W X Y
L	London	A B C D E F G H J K L M N O P R S T U V W X Y
M	Manchester	A–Y Note: MN and MAN reserved for **Isle of Man**
N	Newcastle	A B C D E G H J K L M N O (NF is not issued) P R S T U V W X Y
O	Oxford	A–Y
P	Preston	A B C D E F G H J K L M N O P R S T
	Carlisle	U V W X Y
R	Reading	A–Y
	Glasgow	A B C D E F G H J
S	Edinburgh	K L M N O
	Dundee	P R S T
	Aberdeen	U V W

	Inverness	X Y
V	Worcester	A–Y
	Exeter	A B C D E F G H J
W	Truro	K L
	Bristol	M N O P R S T U V W X Y
	Leeds	A B C D E F G H J K
Y	Sheffield	L M N O P R S T U V W X Y Z

The data above only applies to cars registered after 2000.
Therefore only collect number plates that have two letters at the front AND one of the following numbers.
51, 02, 52, 03, 53, 04, 54, 05, 55, 06, 56, 07, 57, 08, 58, 09, 59, 10, 60, 11, 61, 12, 62, 13, 63, 14, or 64.

There is a map on the next page with all the places on them. Measure the distance, from where you are, to the place the car came from and see how far it is.

The scale is 1 millimetre = 4 miles.

Keep a count of the results as shown below.

Distance in miles

Up to 100	100 – 200	200 – 300	300 – 400	400 – 500	Over 500

Once the data is completed draw a pie chart to show the above results.

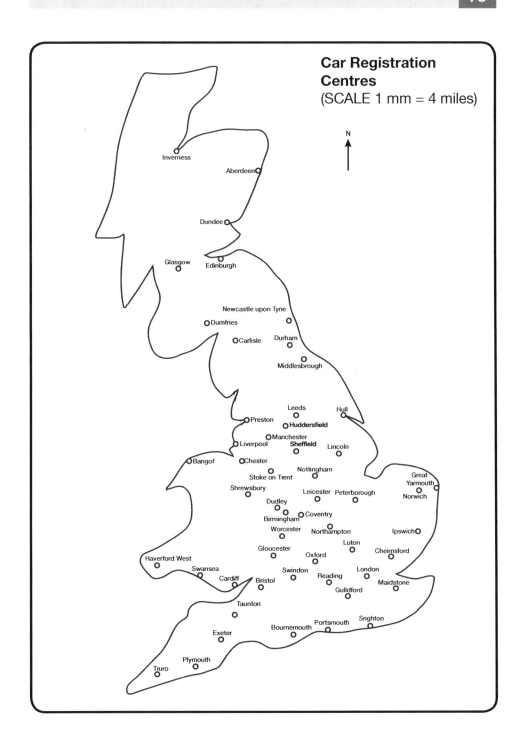

Car Registration Centres
(SCALE 1 mm = 4 miles)

CHAPTER 8

Adding and Subtracting Decimals

8. ADDING AND SUBTRACTING DECIMALS

What is a DECIMAL POINT?

In money, a decimal point separates the pounds from the pence: £12.48

In length, it separates the metres from the centimeters: 3.58 metres.

This is called a **decimal point** – a separator.
It is used to separate larger things from smaller things. It separates pounds (big) from pence (smaller). It separates hours (big) from minutes (smaller).

In numbers, it separates whole ones (big) from bits that are less than whole ones (smaller).
It is necessary to keep different things apart.
You can't add 5 battles and 3 ships to get 8 battleships – it is nonsense.

Similarly you can't add 5 whole ones and 3 bits to get 8 whole bits – also nonsense.
You have to keep the different things apart and that is what the decimal point does.

For example: 3.17 means 3 whole ones and 17 small pieces. (How big the pieces are does not matter – they are not big enough to make another whole one.)

17.305 means 17 whole ones and 305 bits that are not big enough to make another whole one.

All that is necessary when adding or subtracting decimals is to make sure that the whole ones are kept separate from the bits. You can add whole ones together and you can add bits together, but you can't add different things together.

For example 12.7 + 4.2

If the decimal points are lined up underneath each other, then all the whole ones are on the left and all the bits are on the right.

12.73　　The decimal points are lined up underneath each other.
　4.2　　All the whole ones are on the left and all the bits are on the right.

Now we can add them up.

The decimal point in the answer will go directly underneath the others, so that can be put in straight away.

12.73
4.2
____
.

The decimal point in the answer has been inserted, so just add the columns up as usual.

12.73
4.2
____
16.93 **Answer**

Its as **easy** as that!
But note the **tidiness**. Columns nicely under each other.

Do exactly the same thing for subtraction.

For example **24.56 – 17.2**

24.56
-17.2

Line the decimal points up underneath each other

24.56
-17.2
_____
.

Put the decimal point in the answer and then subtract

24.56
-17.2
_____
7.36 **Answer**

Once again... Keep it tidy!

Where is the decimal point in 53?
There **is** one. Or at least there **should** be.
53 is really **53.0** (53 whole ones and 0 bits).

Mathematicians, however, tend to be a bit lazy and if there aren't any bits, they leave off the decimal point and just write 53 instead of 53.0

But it mustn't be left off when adding or subtracting.

For example **9.782 + 124 + 18.6**

9.782
124.0
18.6
_____
.

Put the decimal point in the answer and then add.

9.782
124.0
18.6
_____
152.382

By keeping everything tidy, the columns are kept in the right place.

Answer 152.382

Do exactly the same thing for subtraction.

For example **63.5 – 25**

63.5
25.0   (because 25 is really **25.0**)
  .

Everything is separated properly, so now just subtract as usual.

63.5
25.0
38.5   **Answer**

Exercise 17

1. Calculate the following

a) 14.2 + 8.445 + 9   e) 486 – 83.24
b) 47.193 – 36.02   f) 51.73 – 0.009
c) 361 + 98.001 + 0.1234   g) 56.4567 + 7.12 + 9.7
d) 17 + 6.2 + 340   h) 25.2 + 17.52 – 31.9

For h) do the add part first to get an answer, and then do the subtract part

2. Don't be confused by the £ sign – money is still a decimal. It is quite a
   good idea to leave the £ sign out while doing the calculations and just
   put it back in when you have the answer.
   Be careful with these; there are a few tricky ones.

a) £11.23 + £346.15 + £1.07   f) £291.32 - £17
b) £2.48 + £3.65 + £1.57 + £10.29   g) £23.49 + 65p
c) £1.73 + £58.42 + £7   h) £14.71 - 46p
d) £48.67 - £12.53   i) £38 - £4.86
e) £79.22 - £37.54

3. Now think about this one.
   47 + 29.3 + 1.06 – 3.7

4. What about the next two. Are they too difficult?

    a) **1098345 + 2374.080907 + 239166.1**

    b) **735422.77465 – 84568.33387**

5. OK – now show me how clever you are.

Add the numbers below. Easy? Now see if you can subtract the two numbers.

498723945827215.09283940238

7273645.72634759589367

CHAPTER 9

Statistics

9. STATISTICS

This is all about doing some simple arithmetic with the data that has been collected in a survey.
There are three new terms to understand.

Mean   Add up all of the numbers and divide by how many numbers there are.
Median   The number in the middle **once** they have been put in ascending order.
Mode   The number that occurs the most number of times.

NOTE. The **mean** is also called the **average**.

These three words are used to describe a set of data.

For example. 3, 1, 5, 7, 5, 2, 9, 4, 3, 8, 2, 1, 3, 4, 3
Suppose the above numbers were the hours of overtime put in by 15 workers.

Mean = add them all up and divide by 15 (there are 15 workers).
That comes to 60 ÷ 15 which is 4.
The mean is 4. (4 hours)
Mode = the one that occurs most often.
Mode = 3 (3 hours) because there are 4 threes in the data
Median = put the data in order first
1, 1, 2, 2, 3, 3, 3, 3, 4, 4, 5, 5, 7, 8, 9

Now take the one in the middle which is this one.
Median = 3 (3 hours)

OK! So what use is all that?
It is meant to help give an overall impression of the data.

Take the National average earnings as quoted by Government bodies.

This is approximately £26,000 per year.

That means the average person earns £26,000 per year.
But the mean (or average) can be misleading because this figure includes all those people who earn millions. Footballers, film stars, pop singers etc.

Take a look at the figures below for wages in an engineering firm.

Company Director   £72,000
Managing Director   £42,000   These are the wages per year
1 foreman   £24,000

5 fitters	£20,000	each
2 Delivery men	£19,000	each
1 cleaner	£10,000	

To find the mean add them all up, and divide by how many people there are.

£72,000
£42,000
£24,000
£100,000 (5 x 20,000 as there are 5 fitters)
£38,000 (2 x 19,000 as there are 2 delivery men)
£10,000

The total is £286,000. Now divide by 11 as there are 11 people altogether.

£286,000 ÷ 11 = £26,000

This suggests that the average person in the firm earns £26,000 per year.
But, in actual fact, there are only 2 people who earn that much (or more).

The mean (or average) can give a distorted view of the situation.

The **Mode** is £20,000 because that figure occurs most often (5 times) and that gives a much fairer picture of what people working for the firm could expect to get.

Put the wages in order and then take the middle one.

10000, 19000, 19000, 20000, 20000, 20000, 20000, 20000, 24000, 42000, 72000

The **Median** is also £20,000 which is also a fairer picture

So statistics can give an unfair picture of the real situation.
In the case of wages the Government wants to paint the best picture so it uses the Average (or Mean).

There is a famous saying which says there are:

Lies, damned lies and statistics

This suggests that statistics can be the worst form of lies; and it **can**.

Another statistical trick is to say "7 out of 10 people can't tell the difference between margarine and butter".
If this was a genuine test and the results were correct, then fair enough.

Now we don't know if it is true, or not, but we was told that what happens is you go into a room and are given a small biscuit with either margarine or butter on it. But then, we was told, they slapped fish paste all over it! Fish paste would hide the taste of anything else so it would have been a very unfair test.

Unfortunately statistics makes it very easy to cheat.

Suppose you wanted to show that "most people who come here, come by train". You could conduct the survey right outside the train station.

To show that English people are stronger than Welsh people, get English men to lift weights and then get Welsh girls to lift them. Obviously the English men would be able to lift more than the girls.

The point is, **don't trust** that sort of statement **unless** you are given the **full** details of how the survey was carried out.

It has been shown that an "average wage" is not a reliable pointer to what most people earn because it includes all the extremely rich people who earn millions.

However, we do need to be able to use Mean, Mode and Median, so let's do some.

The following is a list of runs scored by a batsman in 9 cricket matches.

0, 0, 2, 1, 5, 20, 6, 0, 2

Calculate the Mean, Mode and Median.

Mean. Add them all up and divide by 9 (because there are 9 scores).
$36 \div 9 = 4$
Mean (or average) = 4

Mode is 0 because 0 occurs more than any other number.
Mode = 0

Median. First put the scores in order.

0, 0, 0, 1, 2, 2, 5, 6, 20

Now take the one in the middle
Median = 2

This gives 3 different answers and the question is "Which is the fairest answer.

Which gives the best picture of the batsman's results?"

The cricket club might think that either the Mode or the Median are the best indicators of what the batsman is likely to score in future matches.

The batsman would rather use the Mean because it puts him in a slightly better light.

This is why statistics have to be taken with a pinch of salt. It can give different views of the same data.

A point about the Median.
It is possible that there **isn't one** in the middle. **Then what?**

0, 1, 3, 5,|6, 6, 9, 12

This is the middle and there isn't a number here.

0, 1, 3, 5, 6, 6, 9, 12

Take the two numbers in the middle – add them up and divide by 2.
The two numbers in the middle are 5 and 6 (there are 3 numbers on the left and 3 numbers on the right).
Add them up and divide by 2

$$11 \div 2 = 5\frac{1}{2}$$

Median $= 5\frac{1}{2}$

Exercise 18

Calculate the Mean, Mode and Median in the following cases.

1. Test marks. 1, 5, 4, 3, 7, 3, 8, 4, 3, 5, 7, 6, 9, 9, 5, 4, 8, 3, 1
2. Dart scores. 120, 100, 26, 180, 26, 28
3. Weights lifted by 7 people. 100, 115, 82, 230, 65, 120, 100

That is easy enough, but there are one or two things examiners can do to make you think a bit.

In the car park below J=Jaguar, A=Audi, B=Bentley, M=Mercedes, R=Rolls Royce

J	J	A	A	M	J	B	J
A	B	R	J	B	R	M	B

16 cars parked as above.

What is the Mode (called the Modal car)?
Answer. The modal car is **Jaguar** (there are 5 of them).

Now to think a bit.
One car drives off and another one parks in the empty space.
The mode is now different. What car drove off and what car parked in its place?

At the moment the modal car is Jaguar so one of them must drive away.
Now there are 4 Jaguars and 4 Bentleys.

If another Bentley arrived there would be 5 and then Bentley would be the modal car.

Answer. A **Jaguar drives off** and a **Bentley parks** in its place.
Another type of problem.
Remember that to find the mean (or average) you add all the numbers up and divide by how many there are.
If the numbers add up to 240 and there were 8 numbers, then the mean is 240 ÷ 8.

Mean = 30

But it can also be worked backwards!
8 x 30 = 240
If you multiply the mean by how many there were, you get back to what they all added up to.
That enables question like the following to be asked.

12 people took a test and their mean score was 15.
One person's mark was lost but it is known that the other 11 scores added up to 170. What did the other person score?

Total marks scored by all 12 people= 15 x 12 (mean x how many people there were).

15 x 12 = 180. If 11 scores added up to 170, then the other person scored 10 to make the total for all 12 of them add up to 180.

Answer the other person scored 10.

Exercise 19

1. The following are coloured pencils.

    R=red, Y=yellow, B=black, G=green and P=purple

    The pencils are laid out as below.

    R, G, B, P, Y, G, B, P, R, Y, G, G, B, P, G, P, R

    Red pencils are added to the pile until Red is the Mode.

    What is the least amount of Yellow pencils needed to make Yellow the mode now that the Red pencils have been added?

2. The mean weight of 9 babies was 7 lbs.

    The weight of twins was lost but it is known the other 7 babies weighed 51 lbs in total.

    The twins both weighed the same. What was their weight?

We will come back to this later on when we have learnt a few more things.

CHAPTER 10

Currency Exchange

10. CURRENCY EXCHANGE

Currency is money. The British currency is Sterling pounds (£). The American currency is US dollars ($). The Spanish currency is Pesetas. Or it **used** to be before Spain joined the Eurozone.

In this chapter, we have left the currencies as they were before the Eurozone was started because it is more fun to use different currencies instead of just using Euros for everything.

Of course, if you went abroad to China or India or other places, then you would have to change your money into their currency. It would all work the same way as the examples demonstrate in this chapter.

Imagine you are going to Italy.
You will have to buy some **Lire** (that is the name of the old Italian currency).

The diagram below shows how to change British money into Italian money, and how to change Italian money into British money.

£	Amount	Lire
0.00	1	2360
0.00	10	23600
0.02	50	118000
0.04	100	236000
0.21	500	1180000
0.32	750	1770000
0.42	1000	2360000
1.06	2500	5900000
2.12	5000	11800000
4.24	10000	23600000

How to use the table:

Always start with a number in the centre column.
If you move right you are changing Pounds to Lire.
If you move left you are changing Lire to Pounds.

Start with the 50 in the centre column and move left to the amount under the £ sign. This is 2 pence. So 50 Lire is only worth 2 pence!

If you start with the same 50 in the centre column, but this time move right to the amount under the Lire sign, you will find the number 118000.
So £50 is worth 118000 Lire (L118000).

Suppose you wanted to take £180 on holiday to Italy.
How many Lire would you get for it?

There isn't 180 in the middle column so it is necessary to add up separate numbers until it comes to 180 altogether.

You can use the centre column to do this by using the 100, the 50 and 3 of the 10's.

£		Amount	Lire
0.00		1	2360
0.00	3 of these	10	23600
0.02	1 of these	50	118000
0.04	1 of these	100	236000
0.21		500	1180000
0.32		750	1770000
0.42		1000	2360000
1.06		2500	5900000
2.12		5000	11800000
4.24		10000	23600000

Add the answers up
```
  23600
  23600
  23600
 118000
 236000
 424800
```
Answer £180 is worth **424800 Lire**

If you came back from holiday with 3720 Lire, how much would you get for it when you changed it back to British money?

Once again the number 3720 is not in the centre column, so it has to be done a bit at a time until the total is 3720.

£	Amount		Lire
0.00	1		2360
0.00	10	2 of these	23600
0.02	50		118000
0.04	100	2 of these	236000
0.21	500		1180000
0.32	750		1770000
0.42	1000	1 of these	2360000
1.06	2500	1 of these	5900000
2.12	5000		11800000
4.24	10000		23600000

Now add them up

```
          0.00
          0.00
          0.04
          0.04
          0.42
          1.06
          ----
          1.56    Answer  you would get £1.56 back
```

The method is always the same. Start in the middle column every time.
If you want to change to Lire, then move to the right (the Lire column).
If you want to change to Pounds, then move to the left (the £s column).

What your money is worth in different currencies.

£	Amount	Schillings
0.04	1	24
0.21	5	120
0.42	10	240
2.08	50	1201
4.16	100	2402
20.82	500	12010
31.22	750	18015
41.63	1000	24020
104.08	2500	60050
208.16	5000	120100
312.24	7500	180150
416.32	10000	240200

Austrian
Schillings

£	Amount	Francs	
0.01	1	70	
0.07	5	352	
0.14	10	704	
0.71	50	3520	
1.42	100	7040	**Belgian**
7.10	500	35200	**Francs**
10.65	750	52800	
14.20	1000	70400	
35.51	2500	176000	
71.02	5000	352000	
106.53	7500	528000	
142.05	10000	704000	

£	Amount	Francs	
0.09	1	11	
0.46	5	54	
0.92	10	108	
4.61	50	542	
9.23	100	1084	**French**
46.15	500	5418	**Francs**
69.22	750	8126	
92.29	1000	10835	
230.73	2500	27088	
461.47	5000	54175	
692.20	7500	81263	
922.93	10000	108350	

Exercise 20

Change all these prices to British money.

1. A cup of coffee

    a) Austria   19 Schillings
    b) Italy   500 Lire
    c) Belgium   40 Francs

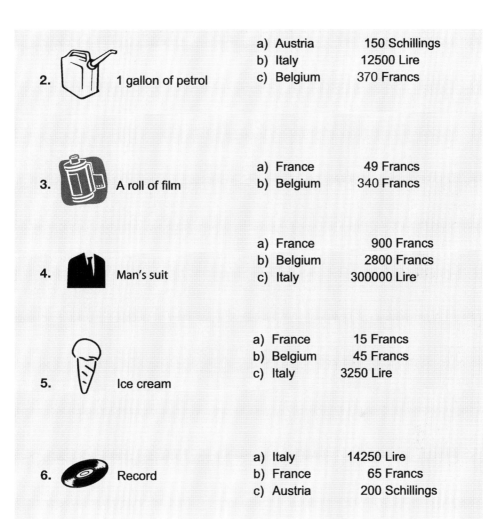

2. 1 gallon of petrol

a) Austria   150 Schillings
b) Italy   12500 Lire
c) Belgium   370 Francs

3. A roll of film

a) France   49 Francs
b) Belgium   340 Francs

4. Man's suit

a) France   900 Francs
b) Belgium   2800 Francs
c) Italy   300000 Lire

5. Ice cream

a) France   15 Francs
b) Belgium   45 Francs
c) Italy   3250 Lire

6. Record

a) Italy   14250 Lire
b) France   65 Francs
c) Austria   200 Schillings

CHAPTER 11

Buying a Meal Abroad

11. BUYING A MEAL ABROAD

Here are two foreign menus. One is from a restaurant in Italy and the other is from a restaurant in France.

TRATTORIA   VENTIMIGLIA

	LIRE
Zuppa di cipolla	3900
Zuppa di cosa	5940
Stracciatell	4050
Zuppa Pavese	3560
Minestrone alla Fiorentina	5170

Fonduta	16650
Vitello Valdostana	17630
Porchetta	16716
Pizza frutti di mare	19800
Fegato alla Veneziana	18920
Bistecca alla Fiorentina	16875
Cordula	8400
Calamaretta alla sarda	18860
Patate fritte	6300

Castagnaccio	6020
Cannariculi	4185
Cassata	8600
Panettone	7482
Insulata di frutta	9600

Caffe/tazza	1080
Vino/bicchiere	2025

RESTAURANT MERVEILLEUX

Francs

Consommé 16
Bisque de homard... 30
Puré e de tomate.. 27

Entrecôte, petit pois,
   pommes mousseline 75
Gigot d'agneau, haricot verts,
   pommes de terre rôties 102
Canard a l'orange 85
Omelette aux champignons............................. 58
Escargots 51

Gâteau aux chocolat 17
Crèmes glacées 32
Macédoine de fruits 45
Riz au lait.. 27

Café/tasse 9
Vin/verre 15

**The menus are, of course, in foreign languages.
Use the provided vocabularies to understand them.**

FRENCH VOCABULARY

Bisque de homard	Lobster soup
Café	Coffee
Canard à l'orange	Duck in orange sauce
Consommé	Clear soup
Crèmes glacés	Ice cream
Entrecôte	Rib of beef
Escargots	Snails
Gâteau au chocolat	Chocolate cake
Gigot d'agneau	Leg of lamb
Haricots verts	Green beans
Macédoine de fruits	Fruit cocktail and cream
Merveilleux	Marvellous
Omelette aux champignons	Mushroom omelette
Petit pois	Sweet green peas
Pommes de terre rôties	Roast potatoes
Pommes mousselines	Mashed potatoes
Portion	Portion (helping)
Purée de tomates	Cream of tomato soup
Riz au lait	Rice pudding
Tasse	Cup
Verre	Glass
Vin	Wine

ITALIAN VOCABULARY

Bicchiere	Glass
Bistecca all Fiorentina	T-bone steak grilled over charcoal and sprinkled with freshly ground black pepper
Caffe	Coffee
Calamaretti alla sarda	Stuffed baby squid
Cannariculi	Ice cream with candied fruit and nuts
Cassata	Fried honey biscuits
Castagnaccio	Chestnut cake
Cordula	Lamb's guts roasted on the spit
Fegato alla Veneziana	Liver thinly sliced and cooked in butter with onions
Fonduta	Casserole with Fontina cheese, milk and egg yolks
Insalata di frutta	Fruit salad
Minestrone alla Fiorentina	Florentine minestrone soup
Panettone	Christmas pudding
Patate fritte	Chips
Pizza frutti di mare	Seafood pizza
Porchetta	Young pig roasted whole
Porzione	Portion (helping)
Stracciatella	Soup into which cheese and egg have been beaten
Tazza	Cup
Trattoria	Restaurant
Vino	Wine
Vitello Valdostana	Veal cutlets stuffed with soft cheese
Zuppa di cipolla	Onion soup with Italian brandy
Zuppa di cozza	Mussel soup with white wine and tomatoes
Zuppa Pavese	Clear soup using spaghetti and bacon

A waiter in TRATIORA VENTIMIGLIA takes an order from 2 English speaking holiday makers.

They both have Onion soup with Italian brandy to start with. For the main course, one has young pig roasted whole, while the other has veal cutlets stuffed with soft cheese. They both have Christmas pudding for dessert and 2 glasses of wine each.

The waiter writes all this down (in Italian) in his notepad.

The order will look similar to the below receipt.

In order to answer these questions, use the currency exchange rates on pages 89 and 90.

TRATTORIA VENTIMIGLIA

Date	Lire
Zuppa di cipolle.........2 porzione	7800
Porchetta	16716
Vitello Valdostana	17630
Panettone.................2 porzione	14964
Vino/bicchiere...........4	8100
Totale	65210

The top line says 2 portions of onion soup.
The price for 2 portions (2 x 3900) has been written at the end of the line.

How much did the meal cost in British money?

Answer on Page 99.

Exercise 21

Write down the following orders as if you were a waiter or waitress (use the correct foreign language). Calculate the cost of the meals in the foreign currency and then see how much the meals would cost in British money.

1. Someone goes into Restaurant Merveilleux and orders clear soup, mushroom omelette, chocolate cake and 2 glasses of wine.

2. A husband and wife decide to have a meal in Trattoria Ventimiglia. The husband has mussel soup with white wine and tomatoes, stuffed baby squid, 2 pieces of chestnut cake and 3 cups of coffee. His wife has minestrone, casserole with Fontina cheese, milk and egg yolks, followed by Christmas pudding and 2 glasses of wine.

3. A family eats at Restaurant Merveilleux.
    The father has lobster soup, rib of beef, sweet green peas, mashed potatoes, rice pudding and a glass of wine.
    The mother has clear soup, duck in orange sauce, fruit cocktail and a cup of coffee.
    The first child has mushroom omelette and 2 ice creams.
    The second child has cream of tomato soup and 1 ice cream.

4. While the above family are still eating, a Frenchman comes in and orders a double helping of snails and 4 glasses of wine.

5. A car load of 6 people go into Trattoyia Ventimiglia. They all have soup into which cheese and egg have been beaten. 4 of them have T-bone steak grilled over charcoal and sprinkled with freshly ground black pepper. One of them has Lamb's guts roasted on the spit and the last one has liver thinly sliced and cooked in butter with onions. For pudding 4 of them have fried honey biscuits and the other 2 have ice cream with candied fruit and nuts. Altogether they drink 6 cups of coffee and 5 glasses of wine.

6. A traveller has no Italian money left but the owner of the Trattoria Ventimiglia says "That's alright, you can pay with British money." The traveller orders a sea food pizza with chips and a fruit salad. How much change will he get from a £20 note?

Answer to earlier problem

Lire		British money
60000	4.24x6=	25.44
5000		2.12
200	0.4x2=	0.08
10		0.00
		27.64

Answer £27.64

Below are two templates for doing the restaurant bills.

Restaurant Merveilleux

TRATTORIA VENTIMIGLIA

Date   Francs

Total

CHAPTER 12

Division of Whole Numbers

12. DIVISION OF WHOLE NUMBERS

This is probably the most difficult part of arithmetic there is.
People say 'I can't understand it. Can I do it my way instead?'

Fine. Except that when they do it their way, they get it wrong!
All that means is that they don't understand their way either!

In fact it is **easy as long as** you follow a few simple rules and keep everything neat
and tidy.

<u>Let us show you!</u>

For example 195 ÷ 15   (a fairly small one to start with).

We are dividing by 15, so let's write down the times table for 15.
You will see why in a minute.

15   30   45   60   75   90   105   120   135

It's quite easy to do that because you just start with 15 and then keep adding 15
until you have 9 answers.

Now for the sum.

15) 1̄9̄5̄   15 into 1 won't go (it goes 0 times). So put a 0 above the 1

$$\frac{0}{15)195}$$ The answer always goes above the number we have reached, and at the
moment we have only reached the first number (1).

So we proceed to the second number.

$$\frac{0}{15)195}$$ 15 into 19 goes 1 time. Put a '1' above the number we have reached (9).

$$\frac{01}{15)195}$$
15   Write the 15 **neatly** under the sum and subtract to find the remainder

$$\frac{01}{15)195}$$
 15   19 − 15 = 4
 4

Now we have dealt with the 1 and the 9 but **not** the 5.
Put the 5 next to the remainder.

```
    01
15)195
    15
    45
```

Now it's a case of 15 into 45 and this is why we wrote down the times table for 15.
Look at the times table above and you will see that 3 x 15 comes to 45 exactly.
Put the answer exactly above the 5 in the original sum because we move along the
sum one number at a time.

```
    013
15) 195
    15
    45
    45        3 x 15 = 45 so write it down and subtract to find the remainder
    00
```

There isn't a remainder so the sum is finished.

$195 \div 15 = 013$
which is 13 because the 0 at the front only means that there are 0 hundreds.

Answer 13

Another example. Follow it carefully.

$777 \div 21$

Start by writing the times table for 21.
21   42   63   84   105   126   147   168   189

```
21) 777        21 into 7 won't go.  Write a 0 above the first 7.
```

```
     0
21) 777        Now it's 21 into 77.  Look at the table above.  It goes 3 times (63)
```

```
    03
21) 777        Write the 3 above the second 7.  Put the answer 63 under the sum.
```

```
    03
21) 777        Subtract to find what is left over.  (77 − 63 = 14)
    63
```

```
    03
21) 777
    63
    14
```
Just the last 7 to deal with. Write it next to the 14

```
    03
21) 777
    63
    147
```
Now it's 21 into 147. The table above shows it goes exactly 7 times.

```
    037
21) 777
    63
    147
```
Write the 7 next to the 3. (Just move to the next space in the answer).

Answer 777 ÷ 21 = 37

You are probably getting the idea by now, but we will do one harder one to finish off.

2,394 ÷ 57

First write down the times table for 57 (up to 9 x 57)

We suggest you do all this without using a calculator because it is work like this that really gets you good at numbers. With practice it just becomes easier and easier.

57   114   171   228   285   342   399   456   513

Start with 57 and keep adding 57 to get the next number.
Use a pencil and paper to add them up because it is easier than doing it in your head.

57) 2394   57 into 2 goes 0 times. Write the 0 above the 2.

```
    0
57) 2394
```
Now its 57 into 23. It goes 0 times.
Write the 0 in the next space of the answer (over the 3).

```
    00
57) 2394
```
Now it's 57 into 239. Look at the table to see it goes 4 times (228).
Write the 4 in the next space of the answer (over the 9).
Write 228 underneath and subtract to find the remainder.

```
  004
57) 2394
  228
   11
```
The remainder is 11. There is still one number to deal with (4).
Write the 4 next to the remainder.

```
  004
57) 2394
  228
  114
```
Now it's 57 into 114. Look at the table to see it goes exactly 2 times.
Write the 2 in the next empty space of the answer.
Write 114 underneath and subtract to see what's left over.

```
  0042
57) 2394
  228
  114
  114
  000
```
Nothing is left over so the sum is finished.

Answer 2394 ÷ 57 = 42

Don't get discouraged if you find this difficult.
It's a big step forward because we are dealing with large numbers and it takes practice to get fully into the swing of it.

The technique is quite easy, but sometimes the numbers can be daunting.

Keep practising and you will reap the benefits.

Exercise 22

1. 360 ÷ 15

2. 360 ÷ 18

3. Out of every 100 homes in Britain, there are 2 that do not have flush toilets. In Greece, the number in every 100 is the answer to 765 ÷ 9

4. Which do you think could move the fastest, a hare or a rhinoceros? The speed of a hare in miles per hour is 540 ÷ 12. The speed of a rhinoceros is 630 ÷ 18. Which is the fastest and by how much?

5. Guess how many homes out of every 100 (in Britain) have a TV. The answer is 1,261 ÷ 13

Mayan Birthdays   e.g. 8th of Pax

My birthday is PAX 8th – when is yours?

The South American Indians (Mayan Indians) had different names for the months and there were 19 of them instead of 12.

The first 18 months were all 20 days long (18 x 20 = 360) and the last one was just 5 days long to make a total of 365 days in the year.
They could not deal with Leap Years.

Here are the names of their months.

1	POP	10	YAX
2	UO	11	ZAC
3	ZIP	12	CEH
4	ZOTZ	13	MAC
5	ZEC	14	KANKIN
6	XUL	15	MUAN
7	YAXKIN	16	PAX
8	MOL	17	KAYAB
9	CHEN	18	CUMKU
		19	UAYEB

Pictures of each month are included at the end of this chapter.

Here's how to change a birthday to South American dates.
Suppose your birthday was September 26th.

First work out how many days this is from the beginning of the year.

January	31
February	28
March	31
April	30
May	31
June	30
July	31
August	31
September	30
October	31

Count the days to your birthday.

Up to here (end of August) is 243 days.

Your birthday is on September 26th so add on 26 to 243.

It is 269 days to your birthday

| November | 30 |
| December | 31 |

Now we know it is 269 days from the beginning of the year to your birthday, it is quite easy to change it to a Mayan date.

Each Mayan month has 20 days in it, so divide 269 by 20 to see how many Mayan months are in 269 days.

```
    013
20)269
    20
    69
    60
     9
```

The working is shown on the left and the answer is 13 with a remainder of 9. That means 13 Mayan months have gone and your birthday is the 9th day of the next month.

The 13th Mayan month is Mac so your birthday is the 9th day of the next month.

Your birthday is KANKIN 9 (or the 9th of KANKIN)

   6. When are the following days in the Mayan calendar?
   Christmas day   New Year's Day   St Valentine's Day

Remainders

All the calculations we have done up to now have worked out exactly (no remainder), except for the Mayan months we have just done.

In real life, most calculations will have a remainder and it is not usually good enough to say the answer is something remainder 23.

If we are doing a divide sum, then the remainder has to be divided as well.

Suppose we were dividing by 24 and the answer was 54 remainder 11.
There are different ways of dealing with this.

The simplest is just to write it as a fraction ($\frac{11}{24}$) because fractions mean divide.

In fact, all fractions really mean divide.

$\frac{11}{24}$ is really $\frac{11}{24}$ but the two dots have been left off.

That is mathematicians being lazy again.

The same applies to all fractions. The '-' line is really another sign for '÷'

$\frac{11}{24}$ is really $\frac{11}{24}$ and this applies to **all** fractions.

So that is the easiest way of dealing with the remainder.
2430 ÷ 57 = 42 remainder 35

Answer = $42\frac{35}{57}$

The other way of doing it is to actually continue the division and get an answer with a decimal point in it.

For example 2536 ÷ 32

Start by jotting down the 32 times table.

32	64	96	128	160	192	224	256	288

$\overline{32)2536}$ 32 into 2 won't go. Put a 0 above the 2.

$\frac{0}{32)2536}$ Now it's 32 into 25 and it still won't go. Put a 0 above the 5.

$\frac{00}{32)2536}$ Now it's 32 into 253. The table shows us it goes 7 times (224). (8 times comes to 256 and is too much.) Put a 7 above the 3.

$\frac{007}{32)2536}$ Put the 224 under the sum and subtract to find the remainder.

```
  007
32)2536      The remainder is 29. We haven't dealt with the 6 yet so write it
  224        next to the remainder.
   29
```

```
  007
32)2536      Now it's 32 into 296. The table shows us it goes 9 times (288)
  224        Write 9 as the next number in the answer (over the 6).
  296
```

```
  0079
32)2536
  224
  296
```
Put 288 at the bottom of the sum and subtract to find the remainder.

```
  0079
32)2536
  224
  296
  288
    8
```
The remainder is just 8. NOW WHAT?
We've reached the end of the sum.
Clever bit. Remember that 2536 is just the same as 2536.00
In fact there could be as many 0's as we like because they don't
count.

So what we do now is change 2536 into 2536.00

```
  0079
32)2536.00
  224
  296
  288
    8
```
Now there is a decimal point in the question we need one
in the answer.
It goes directly above the one in the question
and I have already put it in.
Now we have got more numbers to work with.

So do the usual and put the next number (0) next to the remainder.

```
  0079.
32)2536.00
  224
  296
  288
   80
```
Now its 32 into 80 and the table tells us it goes 2 times (64).

```
  0079.2
32)2536.00
  224
  296
  288
   80
   64
```
Put the 2 in the answer and put the 64 at the bottom of the sum.

Now we can subtract to find the remainder.

```
    0079.2
32)2536.00    Put the 2 in the answer and put the 64 at the bottom of the sum.
   224
    296       The remainder is 16 so we haven't finished yet.
    288
     80       There is another 0 we can use, so write it next to the remainder.
     64
     16
```

```
    0079.2
32)2536.00
   224          Now it's 32 into 160 and the table tells us it goes 5 times (160)
    296
    288
     80
     64
    160
```

```
    0079.25
32)2536.00
   224          Put the 5 as the next number in the answer and put the 160
    296          at the bottom of the sum to find the remainder.
    288
     80
     64
    160
    160
```

There isn't a remainder because 160 – 160 = 0.
Therefore we have finished.

Answer 2536 ÷ 32 = 79.25

Of course it could be that the remainder is **never** zero; so the sum is **never** finished. In that case you will be told to stop when you have reached a certain number of digits after the decimal point.
• 12.6 is just one digit after the decimal point and is called one decimal place.
• 345.73 is two digits after the decimal point and is called two decimal places.
It has taken a lot of writing to explain all this but you would do it much more quickly than we have. You would not write each little step out to explain it. You would do it all in one sum as below.

Exercise 23

Complete the following questions, give your answers in the answer format required.
Always give the answer as a whole number and a decimal (if there is a remainder). Below tells you how many decimal places to work out your answers.

1. 473 ÷ 18   to 1 decimal place
2. 695 ÷ 24   to 2 decimal places
3. 3105 ÷ 16   to 2 decimal places
4. 360 ÷ 16   to 1 decimal place
5. 43291 ÷ 22   to 2 decimal places
6. 345 ÷ 15
7. 1008 ÷ 12
8. 1890 ÷ 30

CEH   CHEN   CUMKU   KANKIN   KAYAN   MAC   MOL   MUAN

PAX   POP   UAZEB   UO   XUL   YAX   YAXKIN   ZAC

ZEC   ZIP   ZOTZ

CHAPTER 13

Multiplying and Dividing Decimals

13. MULTIPLYING AND DIVIDING DECIMALS

You will be required to use decimals in a range of situations, particularly for your exams. For that reason, we will deal with it here, and then we can go on to different work.

Multiplying Decimals

The hardest work has already been done, and we just need a simple way to include decimal points in the work.

And it **is** simple. For example 2.34 x 1.7

Forget all about the decimal points and just do 234 x 17

```
 234
  17
1638
 234
3978
```

That's the answer, EXCEPT for the decimal point.

Count how many digits (numbers) were after the decimal point in the question.

2.34   1.7

one, two three

There are 3 digits after the decimal points in the question, so there must be 3 in the answer.

3978 becomes 3.978

3 digits after the decimal point, so we have finished!

2.34 x 1.7 = 3.978

EASY!

In a test, of course people will try to catch you out.
There are two main ways of doing that.

Here is one way. Calculate 0.23 x 0.014

Forget the decimal points and do 023 x 0014.
That is 23 x 14 because 0s at the front of whole numbers just mean there are no digits there; so leave them out.

```
 23
 14
 92
 23
322
```

As far as the numbers are concerned the answer is 322.
There are 5 digits after the decimal points in the question.

0.23 x 0.014

one two three four five

That leads to a slight problem when you try to put 5 digits after the decimal point in the answer because there aren't 5 digits there.

322

Five four three two one

Never mind – just use 0s so we get .00322
Now there are 5 digits after the decimal point.
.00322 is correct but it looks better if you put a 0 in front of the decimal point.
Answer: 0.23 x 0.014 = 0.00322

Here is the second way of trying to catch you out.
Calculate 5.44 x 17

Forget about the decimal points and just do 544 x 17

```
 544
  17
3803
 544
9248
```

As far as the numbers are concerned the answer is 9248
There are 2 digits after the decimal points in the question.

5.44 x 17

one two

17 has **no** digits after the decimal point (17 is just 17.0 which means nothing after the decimal point)

Answer 5.44 x 17 = 92.48

Exercise 24

Find the answers to the following.

a) 3.2 x 1.5
b) 6.1 x 2.9
c) 12.3 x 7
d) 15.6 x 0.12
e) 3.82 x 1.76

f) 0.58 x 0.9
g) 0.123 x 0.0045
h) 487 x 0.074
i) 6.666 x 12.45
j) 0.00034 x 0.000021

Dividing Decimals

This is almost the same as ordinary long division.

For example 16.08 ÷ 1.2

Start by writing it down just as it is.

$$1.2\overline{)16.08}$$

Now make the number outside the bracket into a whole number. To do that, the decimal point has to be moved one place right to get 12.0 instead of 1.2 (the .0 in 12.0 can, of course be left off).

To balance things up, the same must be done inside the bracket. Move the decimal point one place right to get 160.8
Now write the sum out again with the decimal points in their new places.

$$12\overline{)160.8}$$ Now put the decimal point in the answer before starting to divide. It goes **directly** above the one in the question.

$$12\overline{)160.8}$$ That's the decimal point sorted out so now just divide.

First the 12 times table up to 12 x 9

| 12 | 24 | 36 | 48 | 60 | 72 | 84 | 96 | 108 |

```
  0 .
12)160.8    12 into 1 won't go so put a 0 above the 1.
```

```
 01 .
12)160.8    12 into 16 goes 1 time (1 x 12 =12) so put a 1 above the 6.
```

```
 01 .
12)160.8    Write the 12 at the bottom and subtract to find the remainder.
  12
   4
```

```
 01 .
12)160.8    The next number in the sum is a 0, so write it next to the remainder.
  12
  40
```

```
  013.
12)160.8        Now it's 12 into 40 and this goes 3 times (3 x 12 = 36).
  12            Write the 3 in the answer (above the 0) and write 36 at the bottom.
  ──
  40
  36
```

```
  013.
12)160.8        Subtract to find the remainder.
  12
  ──
  40
  36
  ──
   4
```

```
  013.
12)160.8        The next number in the question is 8.
  12            Write it next to the remainder.
  ──
  40
  36
  ──
  48
```

```
  013.4
12)160.8        Now it's 12 into 48 and this goes 4 times (4 x 12 = 48).
  12            Write the 4 in the answer after the decimal point.
  ──            Write 48 at the bottom.
  40
  36
  ──
  48
  48
```

```
  013.4
12)160.8        Subtract to find the remainder.
  12
  ──
  40
  36
  ──
  48            There is no remainder, so we have finished.
  48
  ──
  00            Answer  16.08 ÷ 1.2 = 13.4
```

Notice how this time we have changed the description of doing it just very slightly. This was done on purpose because if you hadn't **quite** understood before, then hearing the explanation in a **slightly** different way can sometimes make it all become clearer.

In the next chapter, we are going to use just one diagram. You need to be able to identify the different steps involved into achieving the correct answer.

$0.4165 \div 0.17$

$0.17\overline{)0.4165}$

```
    02.45
17)41.65
   34
   ──
   76
   68
   ──
   85
   85
   ──
   00
```

Answer 0.4165 ÷ 0.17 = 2.45

Now write down the steps involvded.

    1. Write the sum just as it was given.
    2. Make the outside number whole by moving the decimal point 2 places right.
    3. Do the same for the number inside. Move the decimal point 2 places right.
    4. 17 into 4 goes 0.

Finish off the list of things we did to get the answer.
The finished list is on **page 118.**

Getting you to explain the steps carried out is an excellent way of getting you to understand the technique, so have a good go at it.

Exercise 25

    1. $1.56 \div 1.2$ 6. $164.22 \div 4.6$
    2. $12.48 \div 2.4$ 7. $0.00224 \div 0.0014$
    3. $5.36 \div 0.8$ 8. $75.696 \div 8.3$
    4. $15.4 \div 0.55$ 9. $171.6 \div 12$
    5. $12.96 \div 3.6$ 10. $1.47 \div 1.5$

Here is a question done by A Hollow.
Mark it and point out any mistakes.

$65.72 \div 5.3$

$5.3 \overline{)65.72}$

$$
\begin{array}{r}
0.124 \\
53\overline{)6.572} \\
53 \\
\hline
127 \\
106 \\
\hline
212 \\
212 \\
\hline
000
\end{array}
$$

Answer $65.72 \div 5.3 = 0.124$

Answer to earlier question

1. Write the sum just as it was given.
2. Make the outside number whole by moving the decimal point 2 places right.
3. Do the same for the number inside. Move the decimal point 2 places right.
4. 17 into 4 goes 0.
5. Write the 0 above the 4.
6. 17 into 41 goes 2 (2 x 17 = 34).
7. Write the 2 in the answer above the 1.
8. Write the 34 underneath 41.
9. Subtract to get the remainder.
10. Remainder is 7.
11. The next number in the sum is 6. Write it next to the remainder.
12. 17 into 76 goes 4 times (4 x 17 = 68).
13. Write the 4 in the answer above the 6.
14. Write 68 underneath 76 to subtract and find the remainder.
15. The remainder is 8.
16. The next number in the sum is 5 so write it next to the remainder.
17. 17 into 85 goes 5 times with no remainder so it is finished.

CHAPTER 14

Banking

14. BANKING

How to write a cheque

Most people need to use a bank at some time in their lives.
Often people find it is easier to have their wages paid directly into a bank.

The most common type of account is the **current account.** Money is put into the account by using a **paying-in slip,** or by having it transferred directly from someone else's account. Money is taken out of the account by writing a **cheque,** or using a **cash-point card.**

Here is a typical cheque.

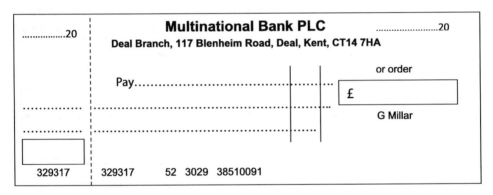

The short section on the left is called the counterfoil. This stays in the book after the cheque has been torn off along the perforations.
The counterfoil (or stub) is used as a record of who each cheque was made out to and how much it was for.

The longer section on the right is the cheque itself. The numbers on the bottom are written in magnetic ink so they can be read by a computer. The slightly funny shapes of the numbers makes it easier for the computer to read them.
329317 is the cheque number and 38510091 is the number of G Millar's account.

A cheque has to be written in a certain way. In the diagram below, a cheque has been made out to pay a garage for some car repairs.

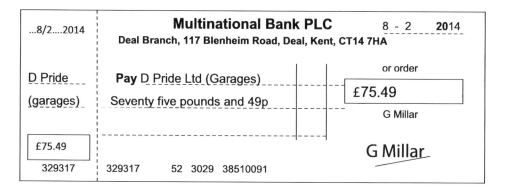

The top line is used for the name of the person, or firm, you want to pay.
The amount of money is written on the 'Pay line'. The pounds must be written in words but the pence should be written as numbers. The amount of money to be paid is also entered into the box on the right (again in numbers). The date is written at the top, the cheque is signed and the counterfoil is filled in.

If you make a mistake it should be crossed out and rewritten, but the mistake must be initialed, otherwise the bank will not accept it. This is to stop someone altering a cheque (they would probably not be able to forge the persons initials properly and the forgery would be discovered).

When there are no pence on the cheque (just pounds) it is a good idea to put the word 'only' after the pounds. This is to stop someone adding some pence of their own. If the word 'only' was not there, it would be very easy to add 99p on the end; or change the two 00s in £84.00 to 9s.

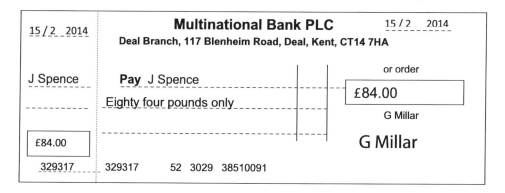

Withdrawing Money From an Account

To take money out of a bank account, make out a cheque to cash.

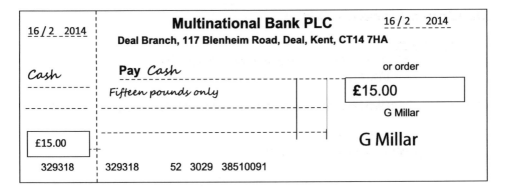

Hand this in at a bank to receive the cash payment.

Depositing Money in an Account

This requires you to fill in a **paying-in slip.**

B a n k g i r o c r e d i t

Date 17/4/2011

Cashier's stamp

52 – 30 – 23

Multinational Bank PLC

Deal Branch

Notes	£50	100.00
	£20	60.00
	£10	50.00
	£5	10.00
Coins	£1	7.00
	Silver	14.25
	Bronze	1.42
	Total cash £	242.67
	Cheques etc.	
No. of cheques etc.		
	£	242.67

Paid in by

G Millar

G MILLAR

564451　52　3023

The following data has to be filled in.

1. The date.
2. The signature of the person who paid the money in.
3. Details of the money. Notes, coins, cheques.

The cashier will check the money and make sure it was added up correctly.

Pretend your name is K Tweed.
Write out a paying in slip for the following.

2 x £10 notes. 5 x £5 notes. 3 x £1 coins. 5 x 50p coins. 3 x 20p coins.
11 x 10p coins. 14 x 5p coins. 21 x 2p coins. 4 x 1p coins.
A cheque for £2.34. A cheque for 1.25 and a postal order for 2.75.

B a n k   g i r o   c r e d i t

Date 23/6/2012

Cashier's stamp

33 – 45– 23

Multinational Bank PLC

Deal Branch

Notes	£50	_____
	£20	_____
	£10	20.00
	£5	25.00
		_____
Coins	£1	3.00
	Silver	4.90
	Bronze	0.4 6
	Total cash £	53.34
		_____
	Cheques etc.	6.34
No. of cheques etc. **3**		
	£	59.70

Paid in by

K Tweed

K TWEED

55672001   33   4523

The cheques plus the postal order came to 6.34 and there are three of them so the number 3 has been entered in the correct space.

Exercise 26

1. It is January 25th 2014. Your name is S Green.
   You wish to draw £15 out of the bank. Write yourself a cheque.

2. It is May 7th 2014. Your name is B Adamson.
   Write a cheque to Consolidated Credit Ltd for £14.52.

   Your boss's name is Mr D Clough and he wants you to pay some money in for him. Write out a paying in slip for the following.

   Notes. 2 x £20. 3 x £10. 12 x £5.
   Coins. 6 x £1. 21 x 50p. 14 x 20p. 17 x 10p. 9 x 5p. 43 x 2p. 19 x 1p.

3. Your name is J Yates and you work for a shop owner named F Bilton.
   It's the end of the day on 9th August 2014 and the till has just been emptied. The following money is put in front of you and you are asked to make out a paying-in slip for it.

   Notes. £20, £5, £5, £10, £5, £5, £20, £5, £5, £10, £10, £5, £10, £5, £5, £10, £10, £20, £20, £5, £5.
   Coins. 10p 20p 10p, 10p, 10p, 5p, 2p, 2p, 2p, 1p, 1p, 20p, £1, 10p, 5p, 2p, 10p, 10p, 5p, 2p, 2p, 1p, 1p, 1p, 1p, 2p, £1, 50p, 10p, 10p, 20p, 10p, 2p, 2p, 10p, 1p, 10p, 10p, 1p, 2p, 20p, 20p, 50p, 20p, 50p, 50p, 20p, 5p, 5p, 2p, 2p, 1p, 1p, 2p, 2p, 2p, 1p, 10p, 10p, 10p, 10p, 20p, 50p, 1p, 2p, 2p, 1p, 1p, 1p, 50p, 20p, 50p, 10p, 10p, 10p, 5p, 2p, 5p, £1, 5p, 10p, 10p, 1p, 2p, 20p, 50p, 10p, 10p, 10p, 5p, 5p, 2p, 1p, 2p, 2p, 2p, 1p.

   Cheques. £7.56, £42.88, £3.90, £4.27

Bank Statements

Statements are forms that show people the state of their account.
It will show **every** transaction that has occurred; all the money that has gone out and all the money that has come in.

The easiest way to explain it is by looking at an example.

Customer's name P. Callaghan

Date	Details		Debits	Credits	Balance
28 June	Balance forward				43.58
29 June	Cheque	812350	8.16		35.42
30 June	Cheque	812351	25.00		10.42
1 July	R&W Printworks			480.20	490.62
2 July	Merch. Credit	SO	12.57		478.05
3 July	Cheque	812352	35.28		442.77
5 July	Mrs Callaghan	TR	50.00		392.77
7 July	Cheque	812353	43.82		348.95
8 July	Cheque	812354	117.50		231.45
11 July	Cheque	812355	26.40		205.05
11 July	Cash/Cheques			14.35	219.40
15 July	Cheque	812356	77.38		142.02
21 July	Cheque	812357	114.00		28.02
23 July	Cash/Cheques			52.17	80.19

The first entry is **Balance forward.** This is the amount that was left at the end of the previous statement.
The next statement P. Callaghan receives will start a Balance forward of £149.57 because that is the amount left at the end of this statement.
Balance means **amount left.**

Debits are amounts of money taken out of the account.
If P. Callaghan writes a cheque for a holiday, the amount will be shown in the Debits column because it has got to come out of the account.
The Balance will be altered so that it shows how much is left after the payment.

The first debit is when P. Callaghan writes a cheque for £8.16. This is taken away from what was in the account and the new balance is £35.42.

The number 812350 is the cheque number. It is written down so that P. Callaghan can check with his stubs to see if it is right.

The next item (another cheque) is also a debit and after the amount has been taken out of the account there is only £10.42 left.

Luckily the next item is a credit. Credits are amounts that come into the account instead of out of it. R&W Printworks has just paid all their worker's wages.
As this money is coming into the account it goes in the **Credits** column and is added to the balance.
The balance is now £490.62.

Then comes another debit. It has been paid to Merch, Credit and has 'SO' in the **details** column.

SO means Standing Order. If you have bills which have to be paid regularly (e.g. hire purchase instalments, rent, etc) you can arrange for the bank to pay these direct from your account. The bank will pay the money every month (or every 3 months, or every 6 months, etc) until you tell them to stop.

Further down the statement there is a payment of £50.00 to Mrs Callaghan.
It has **TR** after it.

TR stands for **transfer.** It is a transfer of money from one account in the bank to another account in the same bank.
£50.00 is being transferred from P Callaghan's account to the account of his wife.

The next 3 items are cheques which P Callaghan has written and the amounts have to come out of his account.

The next entry is a credit. It has been paid into the account, not taken out of it.
Cash or cheques that are paid into an account are put under the heading **Cash/ cheques.** Somebody must have owed P Callaghan £14.35.

The last item on the statement is a paying in slip and comes under the heading Cash/cheques. Anything that comes in is a credit and has to be added to the account.

Exercise 27

Use the following data (next 2 pages) to write out a statement for J Tanner.

Balance forward on 28th June £315.28

```
       Standing  order  form

To                 W Smith & Co
When               7th of every month
Amount             £16.00
Authorising signature        J Tanner
```

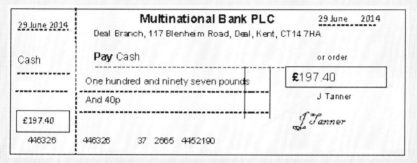

29 June 2014

Cash

£197.40

446326

Multinational Bank PLC   29 June   2014
Deal Branch, 117 Blenheim Road, Deal, Kent, CT14 7HA

Pay Cash   or order

One hundred and ninety seven pounds   **£**197.40

And 40p   J Tanner

                                      J Tanner

446326   37 2665 4452190

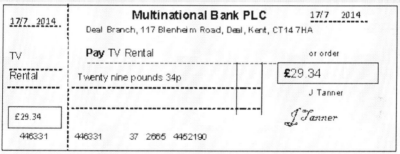

17/7 2014

TV
Rental

£29.34

446331

Multinational Bank PLC   17/7   2014
Deal Branch, 117 Blenheim Road, Deal, Kent, CT14 7HA

Pay TV Rental   or order

Twenty nine pounds 34p   **£**29.34

                                      J Tanner

                                      J Tanner

446331   37 2665 4452190

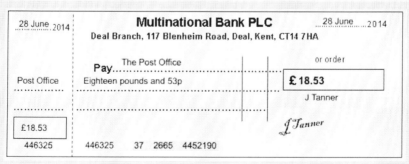

28 June 2014

Post Office

£18.53

446325

Multinational Bank PLC   28 June   2014
Deal Branch, 117 Blenheim Road, Deal, Kent, CT14 7HA

                The Post Office   or order
Pay...........................

Eighteen pounds and 53p   **£ 18.53**

                                      J Tanner

                                      J Tanner

446325   37 2665 4452190

Multinational Bank PLC

21/7 2014

21/7 2014

Deal Branch, 117 Blenheim Road, Deal, Kent, CT14 7HA

Corner

Pay Corner Stores

or order

Stores

Eight pounds 50p

£8.50

£8.50

J Tanner

J Tanner

446333

446333   37 2685 4452190

Multinational Bank PLC

25 July 2014

25 July 2014

Deal Branch, 117 Blenheim Road, Deal, Kent, CT14 7HA

J Tanner

Pay J Tanner

or order

Forty three pounds only

£43.00

R Carter

£43.00

R Carter

634882

634882   21 0399 6726351

Bank giro credit

Date 21st July

Cashier's stamp

52 – 30 – 23

Notes		
£50	
£20	
£10	
£5	

Multinational Bank PLC

Deal Branch

Coins		
£1	
Silver	
Bronze	

Total cash £

Cheques etc.   450.00

No. of cheques etc. 1

£   450.00

Paid in by

Kent Education Aiuthority

564451   52 3023 6726351

CHAPTER 15

Timetables

15. TIMETABLES

Timetables are lists which are arranged by what time something happens.
Timetables can be used to plan events.
For example, you may want to take a journey which involves taking a bus, or a train, or a plane, or **all** three. Using timetables **can** be very confusing.

Railway Timetables

Take a look at the timetable below.
It shows the train times from Holyhead (Wales) to Euston (London).

Monday to Saturday					
Holyhead	Bangor	Llandudno	Colwyn Bay	Rhyl	London
0115	0146	------	------	------	0612
0537	0606	0624	0632	0646	1010
0600	0629	0647	0655	0714	1132
0705	0732	0756	0804	0821	1211
1010	1038	1059	1107	1121	1457
1246	1314	------	------	------	1710
------	1417	1438	1446	1504	1829
1620	1650	1711	1719	1733	2109
1758	1826	1847	1856	1915	2250
Sunday					
0115	0146	------	------	------	0656
1246	1314	1338	1358	1421	1814
1320	1348	1412	1448	1506	1814
1418	1446	1512	1520	1534	1943
1606	1635	1700	1708	1722	2111

If someone caught the ten past 10 train in the morning from Holyhead, what time would they arrive at Euston?

Monday to Saturday					
Holyhead	Bangor	Llandudno	Colwyn Bay	Rhyl	London
0115	0146	------	------	------	0612
0537	0606	0624	0632	0646	1010
0600	0629	0647	0655	0714	1132
0705	0732	0756	0804	0821	1211
1010	1038	1059	1107	1121	1457
1246	1314	------	------	------	1710

Move down the Holyhead column until you come to 1010 and then move right to the time under London Euston.
The answer is 1457

A dash under a station name means the train does not stop there.

If someone leaves Llandudno at twelve minutes past three in the afternoon, what time do they get to Rhyl?

Monday to Saturday					
Holyhead	Bangor	Llandudno	Colwyn Bay	Rhyl	London
0115	0146	------	------	------	0612
0537	0606	0624	0632	0646	1010
0600	0629	0647	0655	0714	1132
0705	0732	0756	0804	0821	1211
1010	1038	1059	1107	1121	1457
1246	1314	------	------	------	1710
------	1417	1438	1446	1504	1829
1620	1650	1711	1719	1733	2109
1758	1826	1847	1856	1915	2250
Sunday					
0115	0146	------	------	------	0656
1246	1314	1338	1358	1421	1814
1320	1348	1412	1448	1506	1814
1418	1446	1512	1520	1534	1943
1606	1635	1700	1708	1722	2111

Turn twelve minutes past three in the afternoon to 24 hour clock time (1512). The only train leaving Llandudno at 1512 is on a Sunday and it gets to Rhyl at 1534.

The timetable on the next page gives the times for travelling in the opposite direction (from Euston to Holyhead).

Monday to Saturday					
London	Rhyl	Colwyn Bay	Llandudno	Bangor	Holyhead
0745	1054	1108	1117	1138	1210
0855	1222	1241	1250	1315	------
1000	------	------	------	1353	1430
1100	1423	1437	1446	1507	1539
1300	1641	1700	1707	1737	1819
1430	1821	1838	1847	1907	1938
1510	1922	1940	1949	2010	2042
1703	2038	2052	2100	2121	2153
1830	2144	2203	2210	2238	------
2050	0030	0045	0054	0114	0150
2145	------	------	------	0210	0243
2200	------	------	------	0153	0220
Sunday					
0845	1320	1339	1350	1404	1435
1250	1710	1729	1740	1808	------
1545	1919	1936	1952	2015	2050
1703	2031	2046	2100	2125	2200
1900	2229	2248	2257	2318	2350

Exercise 28

Be careful to use the timetable which is travelling in the right direction.

1. You arrive at Colwyn Bay at 25 minutes to 8 on a Sunday evening and wish to travel to Bangor. What time do you get there?

2. If someone arrives at Colwyn Bay at 4 0'clock on a Tuesday afternoon, how long do they have to wait for a train to Holyhead?
   What time do they get to Holyhead?

3. Someone arrives at Rhyl at 22 minutes past 7 on Thursday evening. What time did they leave London?

4. How long does the earliest train take from London to Bangor on Sunday?

5. You are travelling from Rhyl to Bangor on a weekday and you arrive at Rhyl station at 1.30pm. How long do you have to wait for the train?

6. It is Saturday. Someone gets on the train at 20 past 4 in the afternoon and gets off again at 19 past 5 pm. Where did they travel from and to?

Hovercraft Timetables

A trip by hovercraft is called a flight. To cross the English Channel by hovercraft, it takes approximately 35 minutes in normal weather conditions.

The table below shows part of a hovercraft timetable, giving the flight times and flight numbers, for the coach, and the hovercraft journey between London and Paris. The trip consists of three parts: by coach to Dover; by hovercraft across the Channel to Calais in France; and by coach from Calais to Paris.

London-Paris

	Departure Days	Flight No.	Depart London	Depart Dover	Arrive Calais	Arrive Paris
1 Jul-21 Jul	Daily	521	08.15	11.00	12.35	17.10
	Daily	524	09.15	12.00	13.35	18.10
	Daily	530	11.15	14.00	15.35	20.10
22 Jul-5 Sep	Daily	521	08.15	11.00	12.35	17.10
	Daily	524	09.15	12.00	13.35	18.10
	Daily	530	11.15	14.00	15.35	20.10
	Fri, Sat, Sun	533	12.15	15.00	16.35	21.10
6 Sep-24 Sep	Fri, Sat, Sun	521	08.15	11.00	12.35	17.10
	Daily	524	09.15	12.00	13.35	18.10
	Daily	530	11.15	14.00	15.35	20.10
25 Sep-22 Oct	Tue, Wed	524	09.15	12.00	12.35	17.10
	Thu, Fri, Sat, Sun, Mon	528	10.45	13.30	14.05	18.40
	Daily	534	12.45	15.30	16.05	20.40
23 Oct-31 Oct	Tue, Wed	524	09.15	12.00	13.35	18.10
	Thu, Fri, Sat, Sun, Mon	528	10.45	13.30	15.05	19.40
	Daily	534	12.45	15.30	17.05	21.40
1 Nov-29 Feb	Daily	527	10.00	13.00	14.35	19.10

NB. French time is 1 hour ahead of British time.
The Channel crossing takes 35 minutes, NOT 1 hour 35 minutes.

Imagine you are travelling from London to Paris on Monday 4th October.
Your flight number is 528. What time do you arrive in Paris and how long was the 6.40 coach trip from Calais?
First find the right date in the above timetable. There are two flights on that day.
The normal daily flight (534) and the additional flight on Monday (528).
The first is flight 528 and the second is flight 534.
You are on flight 528, so look along that line; and you will see the following details.

Leave London at 1045. Leave Dover on the hovercraft at 1330. Arrive at Calais 1405 and get to Paris at 1840.
The coach trip from Calais started at 1405 and ended in Paris at 1840.

Answer the coach trip took **4 hours 35 minutes.**

You have to be careful when calculating time taken.
You can't just subtract the times because the first two digits are hours and the second two digits are minutes. It's the old problem of trying to deal with different things as if they weren't different.

For example. How long is it from 1325 to 1709.

You can't just subtract. 1709 − 1325 = 0484 and you can't have 84 minutes!

The best way to do it is to count up from the lowest time.
From 1325 to the next hour (1400) is **35 minutes.**
Then do the hours. From 1400 to 1700 is **3 hours.**
Finally add on the extra minutes (**9 minutes** from 1709).

Total time = 3 hours + 35 minutes + 9 minutes.
Answer Total time = **3 hours 44 minutes.**

The next page shows a timetable for trips between London and Brussels and also trips between London and Amsterdam.

ALL the timetables in this chapter will be needed to answer the next set of questions.

London–Brussels

Period	Flight No.	Depart London	Depart Dover	Arrive Calais	Arrive Brussels	Departure Days
1 Jul–5 Sep	521	08.15	11.00	12.35	15.30	Daily
	530	11.15	14.00	15.35	18.30	Daily
	538	14.05	16.50	18.25	21.20	Daily
6 Sep–24 Sep	524	09.15	12.00	13.35	16.30	Daily
	530	11.15	14.00	15.35	18.30	Fri, Sat, Sun, Mon*
	538	14.05	16.50	18.25	21.20	Fri, Sat, Sun, Mon*
25 Sep–22 Oct	522	08.45	11.30	12.05	15.00	Mon, Thu, Fri, Sat, Sun
	528	10.45	13.30	14.05	17.00	Mon, Thu, Fri, Sat, Sun
	534	12.45	15.30	16.05	19.00	Tue, Wed
23 Oct–31 Oct	522	08.45	11.30	13.05	16.00	Mon, Thu, Fri, Sat, Sun
	528	10.45	13.30	15.05	18.00	Mon, Thu, Fri, Sat, Sun
	534	12.45	15.30	17.05	20.00	Tue, Wed
1 Nov–29 Feb	527	10.00	13.00	14.35	17.45	Daily

Brussels–London

Flight No.	Depart Brussels	Depart Calais	Arrive Dover	Arrive London	Departure Days
618	09.00	12.00	11.35	14.20	Daily
621	10.00	13.00	12.35	16.20	Daily
630	13.00	16.00	15.35	18.20	Daily
618	09.00	12.00	11.35	14.20	Fri, Sat, Sun, Mon*
621	10.00	13.00	12.35	15.20	Daily
630	13.00	16.00	15.35	18.20	Mon, Thu, Fri, Sat, Sun
619	09.30	12.30	13.05	15.50	Tue, Wed
621	10.00	13.00	13.35	16.20	Mon, Thu, Fri, Sat, Sun
625	11.30	14.30	15.06	17.50	Mon, Thu, Fri, Sat, Sun
622	10.30	13.30	13.06	15.50	Tue, Wed
624	11.00	14.00	13.35	16.20	Mon, Thu, Fri, Sat, Sun
626	12.30	15.30	15.06	17.50	Daily
627	11.45	15.00	14.35	17.20	Daily

London–Amsterdam

Period	Flight No.	Depart London	Depart Dover	Arrive Calais	Arrive Antwerp	Arrive Amst.	Departure Days
1 Jul–5 Sep	521	08.15	11.00	12.35	15.45	18.40	Daily
	530	11.15	14.00	15.35	18.45	21.40	Daily
6 Sep–24 Sep	521	08.15	11.00	12.35	15.45	18.40	Fri, Sat, Sun, Mon*
	530	11.15	14.00	15.35	18.45	21.40	Daily
25 Sep–22 Oct	524	09.15	12.00	13.35	16.45	18.40	Tue, Wed
	528	10.45	13.30	14.05	17.15	20.10	Mon, Thu, Fri, Sat, Sun
23 Oct–31 Oct	534	09.15	12.00	13.35	16.45	19.40	Tue, Wed
	528	10.45	13.30	15.05	18.15	21.10	Mon, Thu, Fri, Sat, Sun
1 Nov–29 Feb	527	10.00	13.00	14.35	17.45	20.40	Daily

Amsterdam–London

Flight No.	Depart Amst.	Depart Antwerp	Depart Calais	Arrive Dover	Arrive London	Departure Days
630	09.45	12.35	16.00	15.35	18.20	Daily
639	12.45	15.35	19.00	18.35	21.20	Daily
630	09.45	12.35	16.00	15.35	18.20	Daily
639	12.15	15.05	19.00	18.35	21.20	Fri, Sat, Sun, Mon*
625	08.15	11.05	14.30	15.05	17.50	Mon, Thu, Fri, Sat, Sun
631	10.15	13.05	16.30	17.05	19.50	Tue, Wed
628	09.15	12.05	15.30	15.05	17.50	Mon, Thu, Fri, Sat, Sun
634	11.15	14.05	17.30	17.05	19.50	Tue, Wed
627	08.45	11.35	15.00	14.35	17.20	Daily

Exercise 29

This exercise is a mixture of train and hovercraft timetables.
Some of them are straightforward but they get trickier towards the end.

1. It is Sept 4th and you wish to travel to Brussels in the afternoon.
    What flight do you catch and how long does the whole journey take?

2. You return from Brussels 3 days later, on a Friday, and catch the earliest flight you can. What time do you get back to London?

3. London – North Wales. How many stations does the last train on a Wednesday from London to Holyhead stop at?
    How long does the journey take?

4. London – North Wales. You live in Rhyl and want to travel to Llandudno on a Saturday. Your friend will get on the train at Colwyn Bay but cannot get to the station before a quarter to 12 midday. What time train will you catch from Rhyl so that you meet your friend when he gets on at Colwyn Bay?

5. London – Amsterdam. You travel to Amsterdam on Friday 25th October. What flight do you take?

6. You return 4 days later, the train is fast, and you get back to London 33 minutes earlier than expected. What time is that?

7. North Wales – London. You are going to a show in London on Monday evening. It takes half an hour to get from Euston station to the theatre and the show starts at half past seven in the evening. What is the latest train you can catch from Colwyn Bay and still get to the show on time?

8. The Paris police arrested a criminal as he got off a coach at 10 past 9 in the evening. He refused to say where in the UK he had come from, but the police found a piece of paper in his pocket which had the following written on it.
    "Train journey lasts 3 hours 50 minutes. Gets to London 4 minutes before the coach leaves."
    Where had he come from?

CHAPTER 16

Car Rallies

16. CAR RALLIES

There are two road maps below to use in the Rally questions.
Follow the clues to get the car to the correct destination.
These sort of rallies are often held by car clubs, with the first person to get to the
destination receiving a small prize.

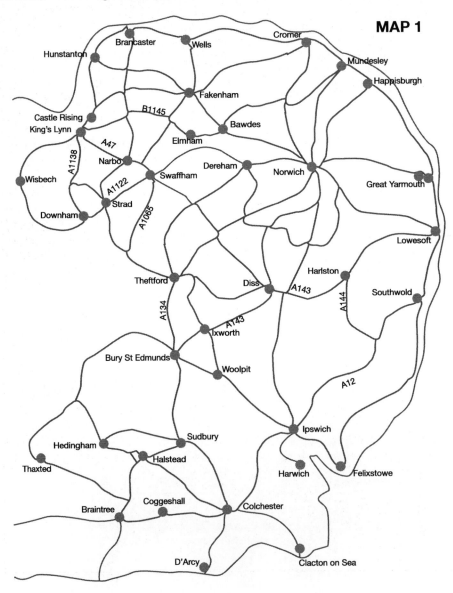

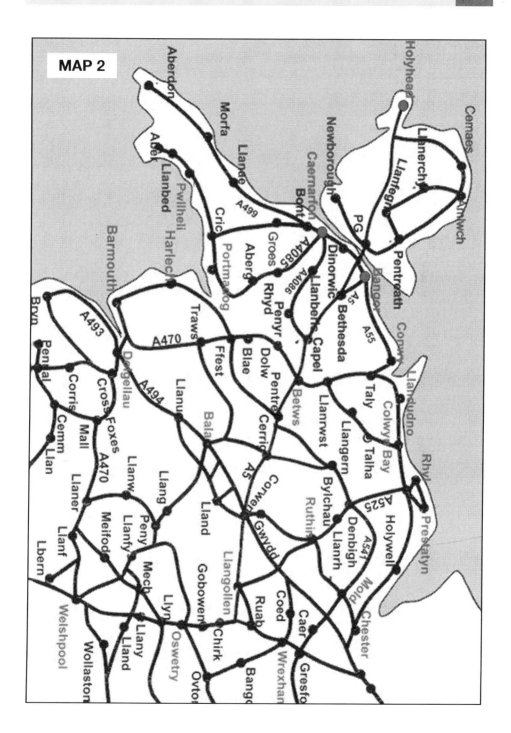

MAP 2

Rally 1 MAP 1
Start at Colchester and drive towards the clever tree. Turn right when you get there and go past the first turning on the left and stop immediately at a farm. You pick 3kg of strawberries at £1.48 per kg and get 56p change from £5.
Now do one of the next two things.
If the change was correct, take the right fork and stop at the next town.
If the change was wrong, take the left fork and stop at the next town.

Now work out how long it is from 0915 to 1111. If this is longer than the time from 1534 to 1738 turn right, otherwise go straight on.
Where are you?

Rally 2 MAP 2
Start at Dolgellau and drive along the road that adds up to 17.

Stop at the second town and work out $\frac{1}{3} + \frac{1}{2}$
Now do one of the next three things.

If the answer is $\frac{2}{5}$ then turn left

If the answer is $\frac{2}{6}$ then turn right

If the answer is $\frac{5}{6}$ then go straight on

Take the third turn on the right and pass through the next town.
Stop at the T junction after the town.

If 90 x 27 is greater than 45 x 53, turn right and stop at the second town, if it isn't, turn left and stop at the first town.
Where are you?

Rally 3 MAP 1
Start at Downham and drive east on the road whose number is 8 minutes before half past 11 in the morning.
Turn left onto the A(1234 -1185) at the second town you come to and drive to the first town.
You see a sign that says "Cream teas £4.75 per person". There are 5 people in your car and you have £23.50.
If you have enough money for the teas, turn left otherwise turn right.
Keep driving to the third on the right...
Your car does 30 miles to the gallon and you have 200 miles to go.
The tank is showing empty. If petrol has to be bought in whole gallons, what is the least number of gallons you will have to buy to be sure of getting there?

If the answer is 6 gallons turn around.
If the answer is 7 gallons then turn right
If the answer is 8 gallons, then go straight on.

Stop at the next town.
Where are you?

Rally 4 MAP 2
Start at Caernarfon and drive along the road whose number is 227 x 18.

When you reach the T junction at the third town work out $1\frac{1}{4}$ x $3\frac{1}{2}$

If the answer is under 4, turn left.
If the answer is over 4, turn right.
Now work out 173.016 + 9.54 + 17
If the answer is 199.556, keep on the same road until you reach the 5th town.
If the answer is not 199.556, turn left after the second town and go to the next place.
Where are you?

Rally 5 MAP 2
Start at Ruthin and drive North along the A525 to the second town.
If 10 to 11 in the evening equals 2250, turn right; otherwise go straight on.
Now work out one and two thirds divided by two and a half.
If the answer is two thirds take the first on the right, otherwise take the second on the left.

If 12 x 65 = 680, turn around and go back to the last town, otherwise carry on to the next town.
Where are you?

Rally 6 MAP 1
Start at Bury St Edmunds and drive north along the A(16 x 12 – 49).
If one and three quarters minus two fifths equals one and seven ninths, turn right at the first town, otherwise turn left.
Take the next left and stop at the next town.
Where are you?

Rally 7 MAP 2
Start at the place that sounds bad (top right hand of map) and drive out on the road that is 19 minutes to 6am.
Work out 39.2 +5.74 + 3
If the answer is 45.24, go to Denbigh.
If the answer is not 45.24, then go to Ruthin.

Now look for a place to the south where the first 3 letters add up to 25 (A=1, B=2 etc.)

Once you have worked out where it is drive there by the shortest route.

Work out how long it is from 1750 to 0615 the next day.

If the answer is 13 hours 25 minutes, turn left.

If the answer is not 13 hours 25 minutes, turn right.

Carry on to the first town.

Where are you?

Rally 8 MAP 1

Start at Hunstanton and head for the building that is getting taller. Keep going until you turn left onto the A(69 x 12 − 781).

Stop at the first town and work out 360 ÷ 15.

If the answer is less than 20 turn right.

If the answer is less than 24 go straight on

If the answer is less than 28 turn left

Continue to 3rd turning on the right.

Now work out how many of the following calculations are correct.

- One and three quarters divided by one third equals five and a quarter.
- 17 divided by 17 = 0.
- 3.7 x 0.12 = 4.44

Now do one of the following three things.

- If one of them is correct, turn right.
- If two of them are correct, take next left.
- If three of them are correct, go straight on.

Stop at the next town

Where are you?

Rally 9 MAP 2

Start at Holyhead. Move out on the A5 and drive your old car to its home.

Carry on along the A5 until you have passed through 5 more towns.

Stop in the centre of the 5th town and do the following.

If 1037 x 259 is less than 2436 x 110, turn left, otherwise turn right.

Drive to the next town.

If 1704 ÷ 12 is the same as 1562 ÷ 11 turn right, otherwise turn left.

Drive to the 2nd town.

If $\frac{1}{4}$ is the same as $\frac{3}{12}$ go to the angry animals otherwise stay where you are.

Where are you?

Rally 10 MAP 1
Start at Ipswich and move north on the dozen road until you meet the dozen dozen road. Follow the dozen dozen road until you turn right onto the dozen dozen -1 road.

Stay on this road until you reach the coast.

Wells is 48 miles away. If a boat travelling at 5 miles per hour could reach it in 9 hours turn left, otherwise turn right.
Stop at the next town.
Where are you?

CHAPTER 17

Multiply and Divide by Multiples of 10

17. MULTIPLY AND DIVIDE BY MULTIPLES OF 10

This is just a short chapter to talk about multiplying and dividing by 10, or 100, or 1,000, or any other number which is followed by zeros.

You will know that 2 x 10 = 20, that 4 x 100 = 400 and 12 x 1,000 = 12,000.

All this amounts to is, moving the decimal point 1, 2 or 3 places to the right.

2 x 10 = 2.0 x 10
If the decimal point is moved 1 place right, you get 20.0, which is just 20.

4 x 100 = 4.0 x 100
If the decimal point is moved 2 places right, you get 400.0, which is just 400.

When you move the decimal point to the right, you may get some holes.
Move the decimal point 2 places right in 4.0 and you get the following.

40▼▼.   The decimal point left a space as it moved (it jumps over the numbers).

All spaces have to be filled with a zero; so 40▼▼. becomes 400. (or just 400).

12 x 1000 = There are 3 zeros; so move the decimal point 3 places right.

12.0 x 1,000 = 120▼▼. The decimal point has moved 3 places right and in doing so, it left two spaces (holes). The ▼ sign is the computer sign for a space.
The spaces have to be filled with zeros; so 12.0 x 1,000 = 12,000.0 (or just 12,000)

More examples

- 47.36 x 1,000 = 4,736▼. Which is 43760. Or 43760
- 2.9 x 100,000 = 29▼▼▼▼. Because the decimal point had to move 5 places. So the answer is 290,000
- 62.93847 x 10,000 is 629,384.7 because the decimal point had to move 4 places.

To multiply by a number that ends in one or more zeros; move the point to the right and fill any spaces that are made with zeros.

Division

This is exactly the opposite.

Just move the decimal point to the left and fill any spaces with zeros.

Examples.

- 38.5 ÷ 1,000 = .▼385 which is 0.0385 (the 0 in front of the decimal point is not necessary but it looks better).
- 2 ÷ 10,000 = 2.0 ÷ 10,000 = .▼▼▼2 which is 0.0002
- 536.7 ÷ 100 = 5.367 (moving the point doesn't leave any spaces this time)

To divide by a number that ends in one or more zeros; move the point to the left and fill any spaces that are made with zeros.

You could, of course, work all these out the long way as we did in Chapter 13.

CHAPTER 18

Percentages and VAT

18. PERCENTAGES AND VAT

This is something else that can be done very easily once two things are understood.

1. 8% just means $\frac{8}{100}$.
   The % sign sort of reminds you because it is just a funny way of writing 100.
   %➞100 (so every time you look at % you should see 100)

2. 'OF' always means 'TIMES'.

Remember these two things and percentages become straightforward.

For example. 8% of 62 is just another way of writing $\frac{8}{100}$ x 62 and this is just a fraction sum that we have already done lots of.

$\frac{8}{100}$ x 62   Write it as a fraction sum and use the arrow method.

$\frac{8}{100}$ x $\frac{62}{1}$ = $\frac{496}{100}$

It takes 100 pieces to make a whole one, so you can get 4 whole ones out of 496 with 96 left over.

Answer. $4\frac{96}{100}$ or just divide by 100 and write it as a decimal **4.96**

Example 35% of 156 means $\frac{35}{100}$ x $\frac{156}{1}$

Work it out $\frac{35}{100}$ x $\frac{156}{1}$ = $\frac{5460}{100}$

Answer 35% of 156 = **54.60**   (OR $54\frac{60}{100}$ which is $54\frac{3}{5}$ when simplified)

An electric eel can give a shock which is 64% of 625 volts.

64% of 625 means $\frac{64}{100}$ x $\frac{625}{1}$

Work it out. $\frac{64}{100}$ x $\frac{625}{1}$ = $\frac{40000}{100}$ and this is 400.

Answer. An electric eel can deliver a shock of **400 volts.**

Money Problems.

It makes **NO** difference. Do **exactly the same** thing

Find 18% of £3.50

18% of £3.50 = $\frac{18}{100}$ x $\frac{3.5}{1}$ = $\frac{63}{100}$ = 0.63

Answer 18% of £3.50 = **£0.63** (or **63 pence**)

There is no need to learn anything different.
Just use the techniques we have already used earlier in this book.

Exam questions often include calculation concerning VAT.

VAT (Value Added Tax) is 20% and has to be added to all bills and purchases.
There are some exclusions but in this work, we will always take VAT to be 20%.

A pair of shoes cost £23 before VAT is added.
What do they cost including VAT?

VAT is 20% so we need to know 20% of £23.

$\frac{20}{100}$ x $\frac{23}{1}$ = $\frac{460}{100}$ = 460.0 ÷ 100 = 4.60

So VAT is £4.60.

Cost of shoes including VAT = £23 + £4.60 = **£27.60**

Exercise 30

Interesting True Facts

1. It would take a snail about 8% of 25 weeks to crawl a mile.
   How long is this?

2. During the last year, Iceland has drifted about 70% of 23 centimetres
   away from Europe. How far is that?

3. The world record for "chinning" (hanging from a bar and pulling yourself

up to touch your chin on the bar) is 85% of 200. How many chins is that?

4. A skydiver with arms outstretched will reach a speed that is 40% of 300 miles per hour. How fast is that?

5. Work out the speed of sound. It is about 95% of 800 miles per hour.

6. If one gooseberry bush produces 18% of 25kg of fruit, how many kilograms could be got from 30 gooseberry bushes.

7. Petrol costs about £6.20 per gallon. The government takes approximately 40% of this. How much does the government take?

8. Add VAT to the following items.
   a) A toy costing £7
   b) A camera costing £468
   c) An electric drill costing £84

Harder Percentages

Even if there are decimal points in both parts of the question, it is still done in exactly the same way.

For example. 8.5% of 5.8
It looks horrible but **just treat it the same way**.

$\frac{8.5}{100} \times \frac{5.8}{1}$ write it out exactly the way we have been writing it out.

Now do the sum. We have already learnt how to multiply decimals.

$$\frac{8.5}{100} \times \frac{5.8}{1} = \frac{49.3}{100}$$

Divide by 100 is easy, so the **answer** is **0.493**

So we just do the same thing **every** time.

Exercise 31

1. Work out the following.

   a) 22% of 35.5   c) 46% of 74.3   e) 70% of 62.8

   b) 12.5% of 45   d) 8.5% of 71   f) 8.5% of 26.2

2. What is the price of a £75.20 phone after VAT has been added?

3. A computer is advertised for £390. What will it cost when VAT is added?

CHAPTER 19

Garage Repairs

19. GARAGE REPAIRS

Cars are very expensive to run. There is a lot that can go wrong with them and they are not cheap to repair.

Things wear out even if the driver is careful.

Tyres, for instance, will last about 20,000 miles and it will cost between £60 and £300 each to replace them (depending on the car).
Normally a driver will take 2 years to go 20,000 miles.

Here is a list of how long things will normally last. A careful driver could make them last longer and a poor driver could wear them out a lot quicker.

Item	How long it lasts
• Brakes	15,000 miles
• Exhaust	2 years
• Tyres	20,000 miles
• Battery	3 years
• Engine	90,000 miles

The above figures are rough ideas.
A large modern car's engine may well last 200,000 miles, and a stainless steel exhaust will last many years.

In this chapter, imagine you are working in the accounts department of a garage and it is your job to work out the price to charge the customer.

It is broken into 2 parts.

1. Labour charge. This is the amount charged for the time the mechanic spent repairing or servicing the car.
2. Parts cost. This is the cost of any spare parts that have to be used.

When a car comes in for work to be done on it, a job card, with a list of the things to be done, will be made out and given to the mechanic.

HUNTER & MARCH
GARAGE LTD

Job No. **3624**   Date **11ᵗʰ December**

Customer **Mr Lombard**

Address **17 Dola Parade**

Car type **B**

Work to be carried out

1. Fit new gearbox
2. Fit new clutch master cylinder

There are three car types.

A is a small car, **B** is a medium car and **C** is a luxury car.

Parts and Materials

Foreman's comments

The mechanic will do the work and, if any spare parts are needed, he will get them from the stores department, who will make a record on the job card of which spare parts were used.

When all the jobs are finished, the card will be given to the foreman who will make any necessary comments and then pass it on to the accounts department.

In order for the accounts department to be able to do their job, they need a list of prices for the spare parts and a list of how many hours labour they can charge.

All car manufacturers supply garages with a list of how long each job should take and this is the most the garage is allowed to charge.
These times are called "Standard Times".

For example, if the standard time to fit a new radiator is $2\frac{1}{2}$ hours, then that is all the garage is allowed to charge for. **But**, there are allowances; if the job takes longer due to broken, or rusted bolts, then extra time can be charged for.

Part	Car Type		
	A	**B**	**C**
Exchange gearbox	£500	£860	£2500
Exchange engine	£2300	£3180	£5300
Spark plug	£6	£7	£8
Contact points	£3.14	£3.14	£3.14
Rocker box gasket	£4	£5.20	£8
Decoke gasket set	£9.25	£12.60	£23.45
Exhaust valve	£8.90	££11.30	£18.50
Brake shoes (or pads)	£30	£40	£60
Fan belt	£13.48	£26.79	£45
Clutch pressure plate	£49	£53	£80
Clutch release bearing	£12.38	£16.77	£32.90
Clutch master cylinder	£53	£72	£112
Rear subframe	£488		
Windscreen	£198	£236	£398
Radiator	£216.67	£348.27	£548.44
Front bumper	£187	£212	£418
Rear bumper	£212	£287.66	£519.38
Petrol tank	£156	£255	£417
Rear light assembly	£187	£243.78	£395.80
Headlamp	£150	£231	£475
Boot lid	£299	£420	£615
Front wing	£288	£399	£487
Front door	£212.76	£400.99	£500
Bonnet	£490	£645	£846
Radiator grille	£205	£316	£487
Oil filter	£6	£7	£8
Engine oil £16/Litre			
Gearbox oil £14/Litre			
Backaxle oil £9/Litre			
Clutch fluid £8/Litre			

Job	Time allowed for different cars. all times in hours.		
	A	**B**	**C**
Fit new gearbox	3	4	5
Fit exchange engine	8	10	15
Tune engine	2	2	2
Decarbonise engine (Decoke)	8	12	16
Fit new clutch	4	5	10
Fit new clutch master cylinder	1	1	2
Reline brakes	2	2	3
Fit new fan belt	$\frac{1}{2}$	$\frac{1}{2}$	1
Fit new radiator	$1\frac{1}{2}$	2	$2\frac{1}{2}$
Fit new rear subframe	10		
Fit new track rod ends	2	2	2
MOT test	$1\frac{1}{4}$	$1\frac{1}{4}$	$1\frac{1}{4}$
Fit new windscreen	2	2	2
12000 mile service	2	$2\frac{1}{2}$	4
24000 mile service	3	3	6

To work out the labour charge, just look up the standard time (above) and multiply by the charge per hour.
The price of the spare parts that were used can be found in the spare parts price list.

Once all these have been worked out, and added up, the customer's bill can be totalled.

Add the labour charge, plus the spare parts charge, and then add VAT at 20%.

All labour charges will be calculated at **£90 per hour** though, in reality, this can vary from about £70 up to £120 per hour.
To see it working, let's take an example.

HUNTER & MARCH
GARAGE LTD

Job No. **3624**   Date **11ᵗʰ December**

Customer **Mr Lombard**

Address **17 Dola Parade**

Car type **B**

Work to be carried out

3. Fit new gearbox
4. Fit new clutch master cylinder

Parts and Materials

Gearbox	2 Litres gearbox oil
Clutch centre plate	$\frac{1}{2}$ Litre clutch fluid
Clutch master cylinder	

Foreman's comments

Add $\frac{1}{2}$ hour to clutch cylinder time due to rusted clip

Add $\frac{3}{4}$ hour to gearbox time for fitting new clutch

This is a type B car.

The standard time for the gearbox is 4 hours but the foreman said to add an extra $\frac{3}{4}$ of an hour. That makes a total of $4\frac{3}{4}$ hours.

The standard time for the clutch master cylinder is 1 hour but the foreman said to add $\frac{1}{2}$ an hour for the extra work done. Total $1\frac{1}{2}$ hours.

Labour is to be charged at £90 per hour and there is a total of $6\frac{1}{4}$ hours ($4\frac{3}{4}$ + $1\frac{1}{2}$)

$6\frac{1}{4}$ x £90 = £562.50

See the finished bill below.

HUNTER & MARCH
GARAGE LTD

Date 11th December
Customer Mr Lombard
Address 17 Dola Parade

Work carried out:-	**Hours**	**Cost**
Fit new gearbox and clutch	$4\frac{3}{4}$	427.50
Fit new clutch master cylinder	$1\frac{1}{2}$	135.00
Total labour charge		562.50

Parts and material

Gearbox	860
Clutch pressure plate	53
clutch master cylinder	72
2 Litres gearbox oil	28
$\frac{1}{2}$ Litre clutch fluid	4

	Total parts cost	1017
	Labour plus parts	1579.50
	VAT at 20%	315.90
	TOTAL	1895.40

Exercise 32

Use the two following job cards to write out a bill for the customers.

HUNTER & MARCH
GARAGE LTD

Job No. **4219**   Date **17th May**

Customer **R Darby**

Address **Blenheim Rd**

Car type **B**

Work to be carried out

Accident repairs

Parts and Materials

Front bumper	Radiator grille
Bonnet	Front wing
Radiator	Headlamp

Foreman's comments
Charge 40 hours labour

HUNTER & MARCH
GARAGE LTD

Job No. **4220**   Date **18th May**

Customer **D Kemp**

Address **The Spinney**

Car type **C**

Work to be carried out

Fit exchange engine

Parts and Materials

Exchange engine	Oil filter
8 spark plugs	7 Litres engine oil

Foreman's comments

CHAPTER 20

Area

20. AREA

Area is all about counting (or calculating) the number of squares it takes to cover a **flat** surface. It is something that occurs in all sorts of places.

1. The label on the side of a tin of paint says how many square metres the paint will cover.
2. Garden fertilizers say how much to use per square metre.
3. Carpet costs so much per square metre.
4. Farms are a certain number of acres and 1 acre is 4840 square yards.
5. Tyre pressures are measured in pounds per square inch.
6. A geography book will tell you that the population of Britain is 650 people per square mile (it is only 289 people per square mile in France.)
7. Wall tiles are sold by the square metre.

Notice that there are all sorts of different sized squares in the above list.
There are square metres, square yards, square inches and square miles.

A square inch is a square whose sides are all 1 inch long.
A square metre is a square whose sides are all 1 metre long.
A square mile is a square whose sides are all 1 mile long.

You can see how **very important** it is to say how big the squares are.

The shape on the left is 5cm by 2cm.

It can be divided into 10 squares which are all 1cm by 1cm.

It is easy to see that the number 10 could easily have been worked out by multiplying the two sides together. 5 x 2 = 10.
Now it is just necessary to say how big the squares are.
The area of the shape is 10 square centimeters.
It is **not** 10 on its own.

Saying the area is 10 is as stupid as saying "Our house has 10".
10 **what?** 10 elephants?

Be precise; say what you mean.

The shape on the left is 70 millimetres by 32 millimetres.
The number of squares in it is 70 x 32.
This comes to 2,240 squares.

The area of the shape is 2,240 square millimetres.
It would normally be written as

2,240 sq mm OR 2,240 mm²

A small 2 at the top means squared.
It is just another maths shorthand way of writing something.

The shape above **could** have been worked out in inches.
It is $2\frac{3}{4}$ inches by $1\frac{1}{4}$ inches.
So the number of squares in it (its area) is $2\frac{3}{4} \times 1\frac{1}{4}$

That's no problem. Look back at Chapter 4 to remind you how to multiply fractions.

$2\frac{3}{4} \times 1\frac{1}{4} = \frac{11}{4} \times \frac{5}{4} = \frac{55}{16} = 3\frac{7}{16}$

Now say how big the squares are.

Answer Area = $3\frac{7}{16}$ square inches

OR $3\frac{7}{16}$ sq in

OR $3\frac{7}{16}$ in²

Exercise 33

1. The fabric used to make a Japanese kimono is 0.5 metres wide by 11 metres long. What is its area?

2. A football pitch can be various sizes. What is the area of one that is 100 metres bt 73 metres?

3. The deck of a large American aircraft carrier is 331 metres by 76.8 metres. What is its area?

Measure the width and the height of the following rectangles and then work out their approximate areas. If you start measuring one side in centimetres, then stick to centimetres for the other side.

4. Use cm

5. Use inches

6. Use mm

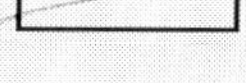

7. Use cm

8. A topo is the old fashioned name given to an area of the size below.

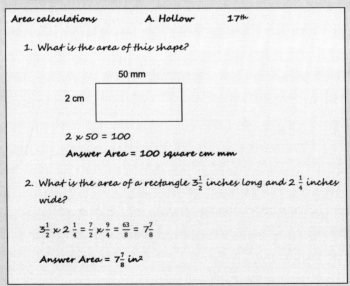

50 metres

73 metres

How many square metres are there in 1 topo?

9. How many topos is the football pitch in question 2?

10. A Hollow has made a mess of his calculations. Mark it for him and highlight his mistakes.

Area calculations   A. Hollow   17th

1. What is the area of this shape?

50 mm

2 cm

2 × 50 = 100

Answer Area = 100 square cm mm

2. What is the area of a rectangle $3\frac{1}{2}$ inches long and $2\frac{1}{4}$ inches wide?

$3\frac{1}{2} \times 2\frac{1}{4} = \frac{7}{2} \times \frac{9}{4} = \frac{63}{8} = 7\frac{7}{8}$

Answer Area = $7\frac{7}{8}$ in²

Area of triangles

Not all shapes divide neatly into squares.
Triangles for example.
How are all the little bits of squares counted?

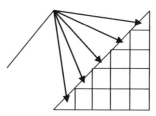

It didn't take mathematicians long to work that one out!

If you stick another triangle on top, then the bit you want
is exactly **half** of the **whole** shape.
Area of the whole shape is base x height (width x height).

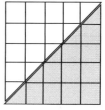

The proper way of saying this is Area of triangle = Base x Height divided by 2.

Area of triangle = $\dfrac{\textbf{base x height}}{2}$

When it is written this way it is called a **Formula**.
A formula is really just a recipe for working something out.

The height of a triangle, or anything else, must be measured **straight** up.

Look at the picture below.
You wouldn't measure someone like this and say they were **12 feet tall**.

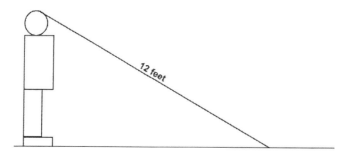

12 feet

Silly isn't it? But that is how some people measure the height of a triangle!

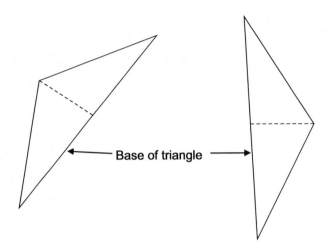

Base of triangle

The dotted lines show the height of the triangles above.

Measure the height from the base to the apex (pointed top) in the shortest way possible.

The base of the triangle on the left is 66 mm and the height is 19 mm

Area of triangle = $\dfrac{\textbf{base x height}}{\textbf{2}}$

Put the numbers in.

Area = $\dfrac{66 \times 19}{2}$

Work out the top line.   66 X 19 = 1254

Now divide by 2 to get the answer. 1254 ÷ 2 = 627

Answer. Area of triangle = **627 mm²** (or 627 sq mm)

Exercise 34

1. The sail of a yacht can be very large. Work out the area of the one below.

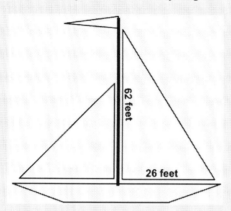

2.

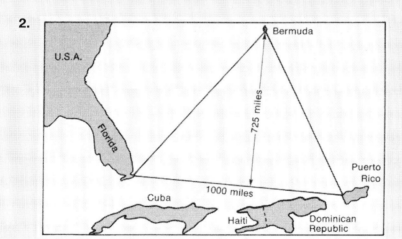

This is an area of sea in which ships are supposed to disappear mysteriously.
It is called the **Bermuda Triangle**.
What is its area?

The next 4 questions require you to measure the triangles yourself.

3. Use cm.

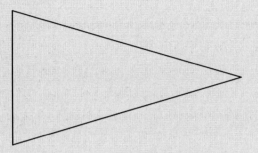

4. Use inches.

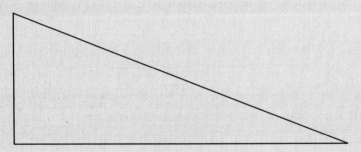

5. Use cm.

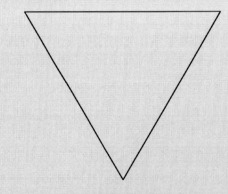

6. Think about this one.
   It is not a rectangle because the corners are not right angles.
   But it could be made into 2 triangles (or even 4 triangles).
   Use cm.

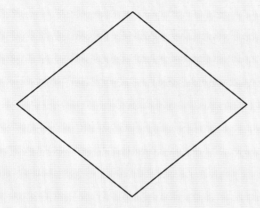

7. What about this one? The area of the triangle was 60cm2.
   The base of the triangle was 30cm.
   How high was the triangle?

8. Answer area of triangle = 24cm^2
   What was the question? (There are a number of possibilities.)

Area of Circle

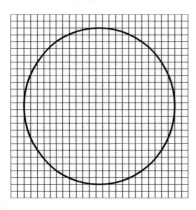

Imagine the problem of trying to count the squares inside this circle!

IMPOSSIBLE! Too many little bits of squares!

Yet that's the problem ancient mathematicians wanted to solve.

It took them hundreds of years to do it!

But, eventually, they found that if you multiplied the radius of the circle (distance from centre to outside edge) by itself and then multiplied the answer by the special number 3.14, they got the correct answer every time.

The number 3.14 is called Pi – spoken as pie – and written as Л.
In fact, 3.14 is not exactly right for Pi, but it is near enough in most cases.

The formula for the area of a circle is area = Л x r x r
The proper mathematics shorthand is Area = Л r²

A formula, if you remember, is just a recipe for working things out.

Example. Find the area of a circle with radius of 4 cm.
Area = Л x r x r
Put the numbers in
Area = 3.14 x 4 x 4
Numbers can only be worked with 2 at a time, so do the east 2 first.
Area = 3.14 x 16

Leave the decimal point out and just do the calculation as in Chapter 13.

```
 314
  16
1884
 314
5024
```

Two digits after the decimal point in the question so 2 in the answer.
Answer Area = 50.24 cm²

Exercise 35

Find the areas of the following circles.

1. Radius 3 cm
2. Radius 12 feet
3. Radius 7 miles
4. Radius 0.5 cm

Unusual shapes

In an exam you may be asked to find the area of an odd shape.
This means you have to split the shape up into smaller shapes, find the area of the smaller shapes and then add them all up.

For example. Find the area of the room below.

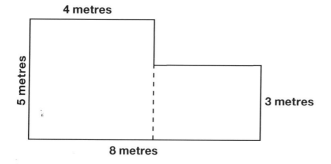

It can easily be broken into 2 smaller pieces A and B.
Area of A = 5 x 4 = 20 m²
Area of B = 3 x 4 = 12 m²

Therefore **area of whole shape** = 20 + 12 = **32 m²**

Shapes can be cut up into as many pieces as necessary.
Some pieces may be rectangles, some may be triangles and some may be circles.

Exercise 36

Find the area of this much more complicated shape.

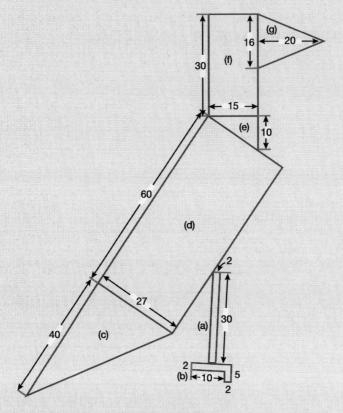

All measurements are in millimeters.

The area has been split into shapes to help.

CHAPTER 21

Holidays

21. HOLIDAYS

Below are some details of holidays and insurance costs for holidays in Paris.
Note that there are different charges depending on the time of year. Things are always a bit cheaper in the winter when not so many people are looking for a holiday.

Holidays in Paris

	January/February					March/December				
Days	*	**	***	****	*****	*	**	***	****	*****
2	180	192	212	250	320	205	230	265	300	345
3	190	200	265	330	410	285	310	335	390	445
4	250	300	355	420	500	370	400	410	480	550
5	340	380	430	490	600	445	490	520	585	620
6	480	530	590	640	700	545	595	610	670	720
7	620	660	705	740	780	635	690	730	770	830

Prices are per person per night assuming 2 people in a room.

Insurance isn't cheap either, but it is essential.
Should anything go wrong, insurance will save you a fortune.

Insurance		
Cost per person		
	Jan/Feb	Mar/Dec
Up to 3 days	£34.90	£40.16
4-5 days	£62.50	£70.28
6-7 days	£85.40	£92.26

There are other costs that may be involved.

1. Optional extras.
   These include things such as
   a) Upgrade to a posher hotel.
   b) Upgrade travel to first class.
   c) Upgrade to Half Board instead of just Bed and Breakfast.
      Half board is Bed, Breakfast and an Evening meal.

2. Excursions.
   Trips to places of interest. In Paris you may want to do the following:
   a) A trip up the Eiffel Tower.
   b) A cruise on the river Seine.
   c) See Paris by night.

3. Single person supplement. If someone is travelling on their own, then there
   will be an extra charge because they will want a room all to themselves.

All these things have to be considered when making holiday arrangements.

Excursions	
Take a trip up the Eiffel Tower.	£65 per person
Cruise on the river Seine (includes lunch)	£98 per person
See Paris by Night. Includes theatre trip.	£80 per person

Optional Extras	
Upgrade to Half Board	£15 per person per night
Upgrade to a better room	£12 per person per night
Upgrade to 1st Class travel	£90 per person each way

Note that upgrading to 1st class travel is £90 on the way out, and another £90 on
the way back.
She also wants to take a trip up the Eiffel Tower and to see Paris by Night.

5 nights in a 5 star hotel in July is £620 (circled in the diagram below).
Insurance = £70.28
Upgrade to half board = £15 x 5 = £75
Eiffel Tower = £65 and Paris by Night = £80.
Total cost = £620 + £70.28 + £75 + £65 + £80
Holiday total = £910.28

£620
£70.28
£75
£65
£80
£910.28

Holidays in Paris

Days	January/February					March/December				
	*	**	***	****	*****	*	**	***	****	*****
2	180	192	212	250	320	205	230	265	300	345
3	190	200	265	330	410	285	310	335	390	445
4	250	300	355	420	500	370	400	410	480	550
5	340	380	430	490	600	445	490	520	585	620
6	480	530	590	640	700	545	595	610	670	720
7	620	660	705	740	780	635	690	730	770	830

Exercise 37

1. Two people go to Paris for 4 days in a 4* hotel in February. Including insurance, they also upgrade to half board and want a cruise on the river Seine.
   Work out the total cost

2. Six people for 7 days in Paris in a 5* hotel, including insurance, in September. 4 of them want to upgrade to half board.
   All 6 want to take ALL the excursions.
   Work out the total cost.

CHAPTER 22

*Bearings
and Treasure*

22. BEARINGS AND TREASURE

The position of several treasure sites is known quite accurately, but no attempt has yet been made to recover anything.
It can only be a matter of time before someone decides to investigate.

We will look at some of these sites later, but first we have to learn how to navigate. That means we need to understand bearings and triangulation.

It might sound difficult but, as you will see, it isn't, **as long** as you follow a few rules. We have already learnt how to use a protractor in the chapter on pie charts so that gives us a good start for this work.

Maps which are designed to be used specifically for navigation purposes are called **Charts** and they will always have North marked on them.

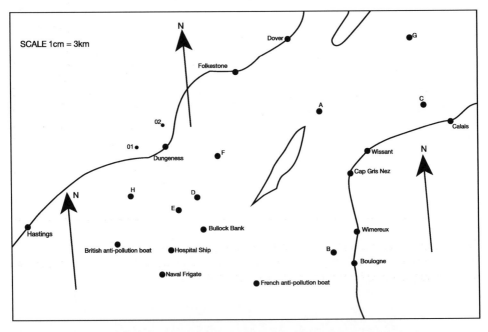

You can see the North line marked on this chart of the English Channel.

In any sort of navigation, it is necessary to take bearings. This involves measuring angles (in the same way as we did for pie charts), but there is one very important difference – the angle is always measured from a line that points directly north. Imagine you are the navigator on a ferry travelling from Dover to Boulogne.

It is your job to give the captain instructions to get there safely – without hitting any sandbanks, or anything else that might be in the way.

Here is how to do it.

Suppose the first leg of the trip is to sail from **Dover** to position **A** in the channel.
Then we need a north line at Dover and there isn't one there.
However, there is a neat little trick that enables us to get one.
We can make a copy of the north line near Folkestone and move it to Dover.

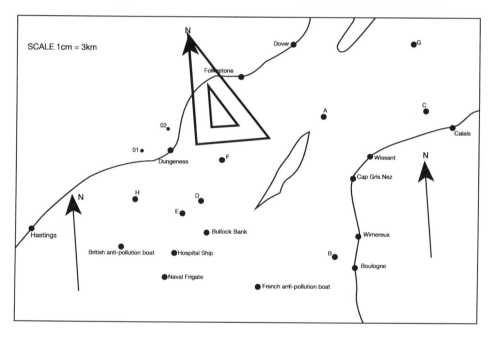

First place a set square, **very** accurately, along an existing north line.
Press the set square firmly so it can't move and place a ruler, or some sort of straight edge, along its bottom edge as shown below.

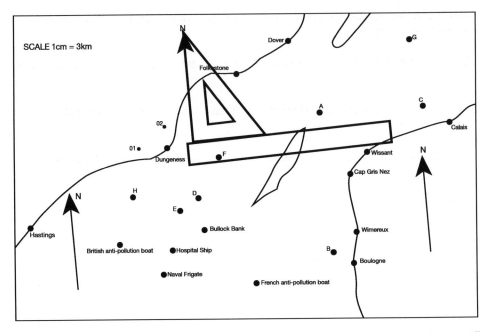

Then press down on the ruler to stop it moving and slide the set square along until it is exactly on the Dover mark.

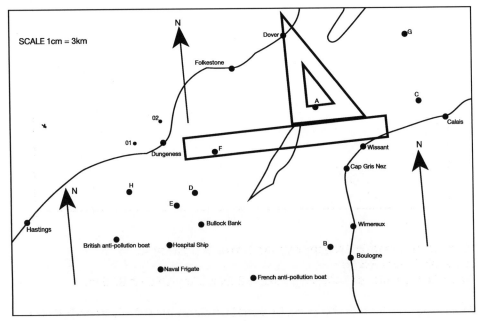

Draw a line through Dover, up the side of the set square, and we have got a north line at Dover! Very clever!

Then we have to draw a line from Dover to the point **A** because that is where we want to get to.

Having done that we put a protractor as shown below to measure the angle. It is near to 170°.

By using the large diagram on the next page you will be able to do it accurately. I made it 161°

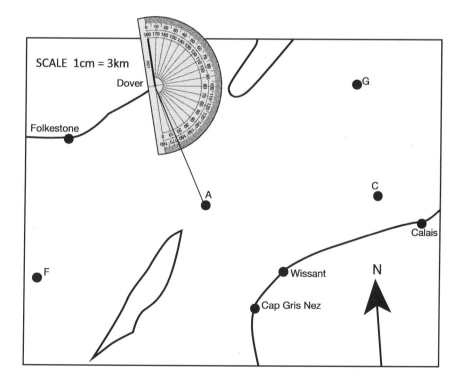

Measure the length of the journey from **Dover** to position **A**.
The scale is 1cm = 3km.
We make the distance 3.25 cm so this is 3.25 x 3 km which is 9.75 km

So the instructions to the captain would be Bearing 161° distance 9.75 km

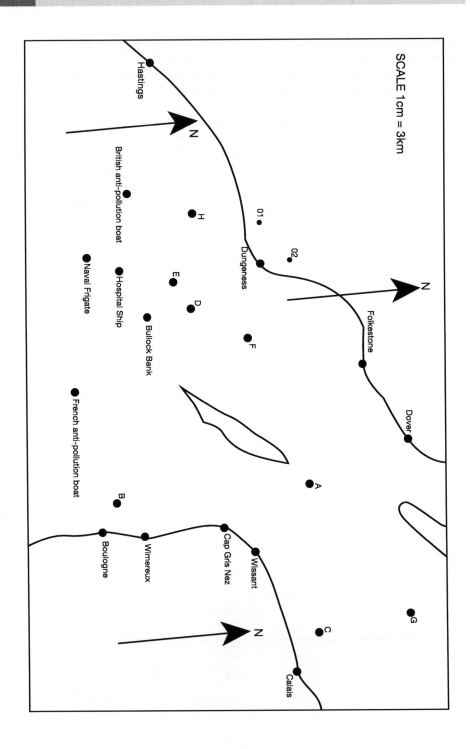

SCALE 1cm = 3km

The ship is going to Boulogne, and the next step is to get to point **B.**
From there the ship will be taken into Boulogne by the Pilot.
This is a seaman who has deep knowledge of the sand banks and other hazards in the area and can easily guide the ship past them all.

To get to point **B**, we need another north line at point **A** because that is the starting point for the second part of the trip.
Then we need to draw a line from point **A** to point **B**.
You have been shown how to move a north line using a set square and a ruler.

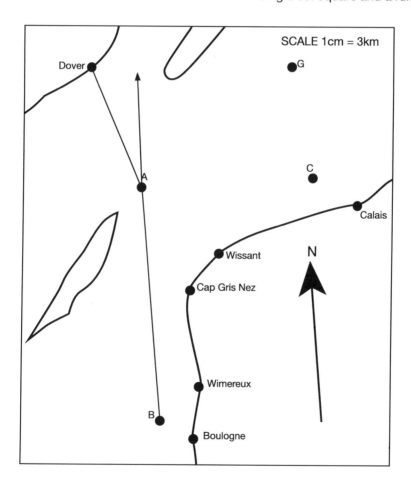

The diagram will be as above once a **north line** has been moved to position **A** and point **A** has been joined to point **B**.

Now we need to put the protractor at point **A** and measure the degrees.

You have been shown how to move a north line using a set square and a ruler.

The next diagram shows the north line at **A**, the line from **A** to **B**, and the **protractor** in place.

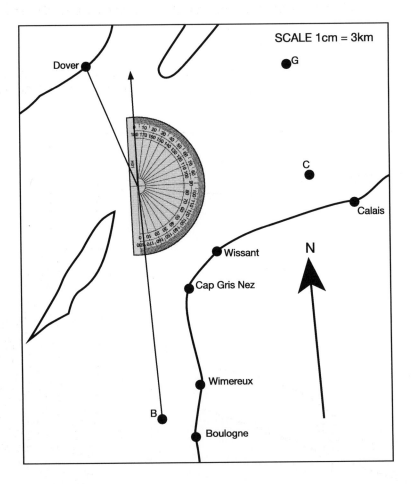

The protractor is showing 179°.
The distance from A to B is 5.5 cm and this means 5.5 x 3 km.

Instructions to captain are "sail on a **bearing of 179°** for a **distance of 16.5 km**".

A bearing can be greater than 180°.
Imagine someone is in a rubber dinghy at point **F** (near Dungeness) and wishes to
set a course for Hastings.

Step 1. Move a north line to the starting point (**F**) by the set square and ruler method.

Step 2. Draw a line to Hastings.

Step 3. Place a protractor on the north line. Unfortunately it doesn't reach the line
we want to travel along to get to Hastings, so make a mark at the 180°
position.

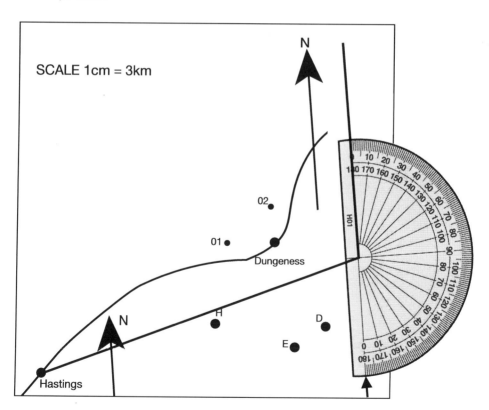

Now turn the protractor around so that the zero is pointing at the mark you made at 180°

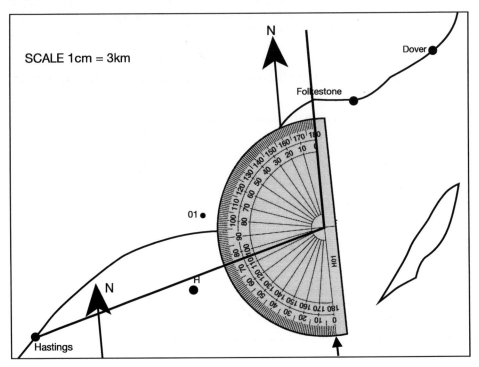

Read the angle from the bottom of the protractor to the line that goes to Hastings. It is 75°. So the total angle to get from position F to Hastings is 180 + 75 = 255°. Measure the line to Hastings and you will find it is 8.75 cm. Multiply by 3 because the scale is 1cm = 3 km. 8.75 x 3 = 26.25

The rubber dinghy must sail on a bearing of 255° for a distance of 26.25 km.

Exercise 38

1. Set course from Dover to point **C** just outside Calais. The pilot will take over from there.

2. A large oil slick has been sighted; and in order to start spraying it, the British anti-pollution boat will sail to point **E** and the French anti-pollution boat will sail to point **D**. Give navigating instructions to both captains.

Other Navigating Methods

An Observer (O2) north of Dungeness spots a sailing boat in trouble on a bearing of 074°. Another Observer (O1) sees the same sailing boat on a bearing of 070° A rescue boat is patrolling at position **F**. Give it instructions to reach the sailing boat.

Before instructions can be given to the rescue boat the position of the sailing boat must be pinpointed.

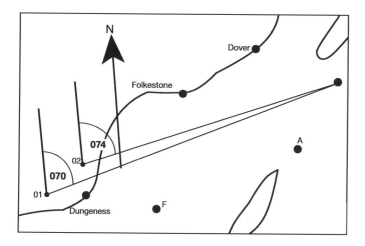

The sailing boat is where the two lines from **O1** and **O2** meet.

Finding a position by this method is called **triangulation**.
Sounds difficult but it's easy really.

Now that the position of the sailing boat is known, we just have to move a north line to point F, measure the angle to the boat, and measure the distance to the boat.

We make it 036° and a distance of 9.6 km. (3.2 cm on the chart)

Answer. Sail on a bearing of 036° for 9.6 km.

Another way of finding a position

A garbled SOS is coming in from 2 ships that have been in collision.
The coastguard at the French town of Wissant only managed to pick up the fact that the accident happened 6 km from Cap Gris Nez before the radio went dead.
Fortunately, a radio amateur at Wimereux phoned up and reported that a faint

distress signal had been picked up on a bearing of 340° from Wimereux and at a distance of about 15 km.

These two bits of information are enough to pinpoint the accident.

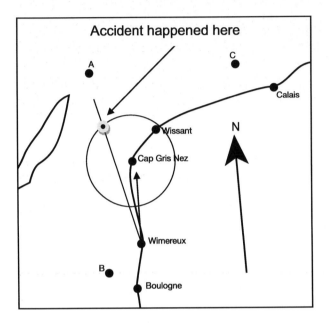

Accident happened here

A circle with a radius of 6 km is drawn with its centre at Cap Gris Nez.
All the points that are 6 km from Cap Gris Nez are on the circle so the accident must have happened **somewhere on** the circle.

The bearing of 340° from Wimereux cuts the circle in two places so the accident **must** have happened in one of those two places.
But the accident was approximately 15 km from Wimereux, so it happened at the second of the two points because the first point is nowhere near 15 km.

Now that the accident has been pinpointed, it is easy to give directions to the Wissant lifeboat.

Answer. Sail on a bearing of 283° for a distance of 6.6 km.

Exercise 39

If you can do this exercise you are ready to find the sunken treasure.

1. A fishing boat at Bullock Bank reports seeing a foreign boat suspected of illegal fishing on a bearing of 015°.
    A second fishing boat at position H reports the same foreigner on a bearing of 060°.
    Find where the foreign boat is and give instructions to the Naval frigate so that it can go and investigate.

The Treasure Ships

There are five maps giving navigational directions to find the position of the sunken ships. It is impossible to be 100% accurate. As long as your answers are **very** close to this answer, that is fine.
Use the clues to find the positions of the wrecks and then answer the questions about bearings and distances.

These are **real** ships.

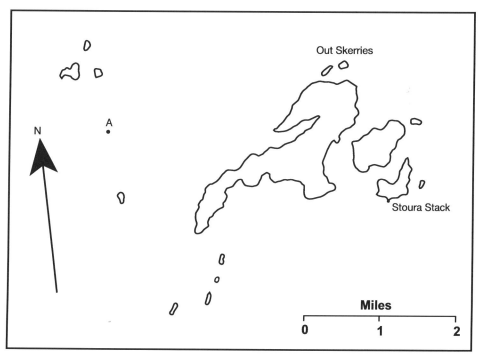

1. The CARMELAN sank 2 miles from **A** on a bearing of 140°
    What is its bearing from Stoura Stack?
    This ship was carrying 3,000,000 Dutch Gilders which would be worth well
    over £1,000,000 today.
    Some diving has taken place but only about half the treasure has been
    recovered.

2. The KENEMERLANDT sank half a mile from Stoura Stack on a bearing of 020°.
    What is its bearing from **A**?
    The ship was carrying coins worth about £45,000. Some of it has been
    recovered but there is probably still £30,000 worth of coins left.

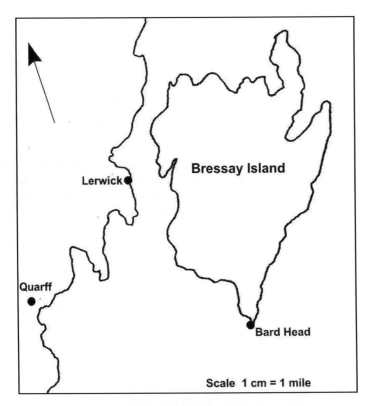

Scale 1 cm = 1 mile

3. The Viking ships **FIFA** and **HIALF** sank $4\frac{3}{4}$ miles from Bard Head and on a
    bearing of 210° from Lerwick. They are more than 3 miles from Lerwick.
    What is their bearing from Quarff?
    Two Viking ships sank on their way home after a plundering raid.
    They were said to be carrying "Rich ornaments".
    No dive has been made on these vessels.

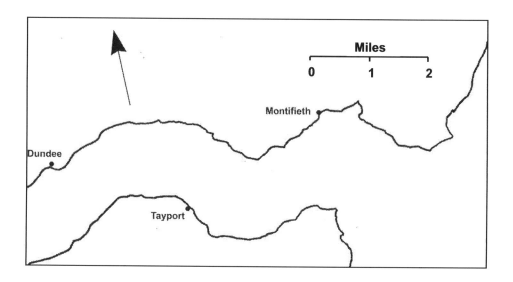

4. The **TREASURE FLEET** sank 2 miles from Montifieth and on a bearing of 105°
   from Tayport. They are further than 2 miles from Tayport.
   What is the bearing of the treasure fleet from Montifieth?
   Dundee was captured in 1651 and a fleet of 60 ships was used to carry away
   the stolen treasure. A storm blew up and sank the fleet at the river mouth.
   There was £250,000 of gold and silver on board but no dive has been carried
   out on these ships, probably because of the shifting sands.

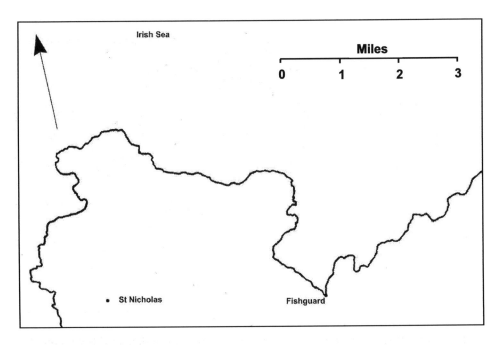

5. The **SANTA CRUZ** sank 3 miles from St Nicholas and on a bearing of 325°
from Fishguard. What is its bearing from St Nicholas?
This is a Spanish treasure galleon which has recently been found and some of
the treasure has been recovered.
She was carrying 220 chests of gold and silver worth at least £1,500,000.

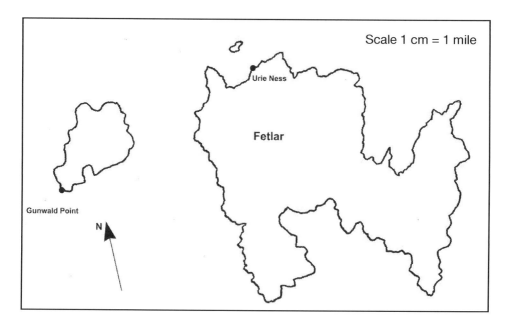

6. Unknown Dutch ship sank on a bearing of 100° from Gunwald Point and at a
    distance of 12.5 miles from Gunwald Point.
    What is its bearing from Urie Ness?

Large quantities of silver coins have been thrown up on the local beach after storms.
There could be a fortune in silver waiting to be found.

CHAPTER 23

Hire Purchase

23. HIRE PURCHASE

Buying goods on hire purchase is certainly not a cheap way to shop.
However, for most people it's the only way they can afford the things they want.

A small deposit is put down and the rest of the money is paid over a long period of time.
It works out more expensive than paying for it all in one go because of the **charges** that are added on.

For example, a refrigerator may cost £380 cash price (that's the cost of an item if you pay for it all in one go) and over £450 with the added charges.

So how is it all worked out?

1. The **deposit.**
    This is a certain amount that is paid at the beginning of the hire purchase agreement. It will be a percentage of the total price but the actual figure will vary in different circumstances.
    A new car may only need 5% deposit, but a very old one may need 50%.

2. The **charge** (or interest).
    After the deposit has been paid the money that is still owed is called the **Balance.**

Let's go back to the refrigerator.
The deposit is 10% (which is £38).
The balance is £380 - £38 which is £342.

The charges are going to be 12% for each year of hire purchase.

$$\frac{12}{100} \times \frac{342}{1} \blacktriangleright \frac{4104}{100} = 41.04$$

12% of £342 is £41.04.

If the hire purchase is over 2 years, then the charges will be **£41.04 x 2 (£82.08).**

The total cost of the refrigerator is the cost price + the charges for 2 years.
Total cost = £380 + £82.08 which is **£462.08**

It is not a cheap way to buy things.

3. The **installments**
    The amount you pay each month is called the monthly installment.
    To find out how much it is, just divide the amount left to pay by 24 (as the hire purchase in this case is for 2 years (or 24 months)).

Amount left to pay = balance + charges = £342 + £82.08 which is **£424.08**

```
        17.67
24)424.08
        24
        184
        168
        160
        144
        168
        168
```

> To calculate monthly payments divide amount left to pay by 24 (because there are 24 months in 2 years)

Monthly installment = £424.08 ÷ 24 which is **£17.67**

Work out the deposit, balance, interest charges and monthly payments for a dining room suite costing £680.
The hire purchase agreement is to be for 3 years and the interest rate is 11%.

Deposit = 10% of £680 = **£68**.
Balance = £680 - £68 = **£612**
Interest charges = 11% of £612 which is £67.32 per year.
Interest charges = £67.32 x 3 = **£201.96**
Amount left to pay = balance + interest charges
Amount left to pay = £612 + £201.96 = **£813.96**
Monthly installment = amount left to pay divided by 36 (36 months in 3 years)
Monthly installment = £813.96 ÷ 36 = **£22.61**

Exercise 40

Work out the monthly payments (installments) in each of the following cases. Interest charges will always be 12% per year.

1. Music centre price £420. Deposit 20%. HP over 2 years.

2. Built in eye-level cooker price £540. Deposit 15%. HP over 3 years.

3. Carpet for hall and stairs price £1,260. Deposit 10%. HP over 3 years.

4. Greenhouse price £360. Deposit 30%. HP over 2 years.

Buying a Car

When buying a car on HP, the amount of interest may depend on the age of the car being bought.

For demonstration purposes, we will assume the following:

1. New car, interest 7%
2. Up to 3 years old interest 8%
3. Over 3 years old interest 11%

Let's take the example of Mr I Pettitt buying a 2 year old Ford Focus for £6,500. He will pay 10% deposit and pay the rest over 2 years. The month is November.

Deposit = 10% of £6500 = $\frac{10}{100}$ x $\frac{6500}{1}$ = $\frac{65000}{100}$ = **£650**

Balance = £6500 - £650 which is **£5850**

Interest charges = 8% of £5850 = $\frac{8}{100}$ x $\frac{5850}{1}$ = $\frac{46800}{100}$ = **£468**

Total charges = £468 x 2 (HP is over 2 years) = **£936**

Amount left to pay = balance + charges = £5,850 + £936 = **£6,786**

Monthly payment = amount left to pay ÷ 24 which is £6,786 ÷ 24 which is **£282.75**

It is now possible to fill in a hire purchase agreement.
They are often called **Schedules.**

SCHEDULE		
Vehicle	**Age**	**Model**
Name of purchaser		
Cash price		£
Deposit		£
Balance		£
Interest		£
balance + interest		£
HP Term		Years
Monthly installments		£
First payment due on 1st day of		

Once the answers have been worked out, it is a simple job to complete the schedule. The first payment is always the 1st day of the month following the purchase.

SCHEDULE

Vehicle   **Age**   **Model**

Name of purchaser

Cash price	£6500
Deposit	£650
Balance	£5850
Interest	£936
balance + interest	£6786
HP Term	**Years** 2
Monthly installments	£282.75

First payment due on 1st day of December

HUNTER & MARCH

Quality used cars

Vauxhall Cavalier 18 years old 102000 miles	£650
Seat Leon 4 years old. 31000 miles. Superb condition	£9500
Rover 45 10 years old. 76000 miles Full MOT Excellent condition for age.	£875
Ford Granada Ghia 23 years old/ ONLY 46000 miles. Must be seen to believe condition	£1490
Honda Civic 8 years old. 90000 miles. Good condition	£3750
Rolls Royce Silver Shadow. 42 years old. Amazing car! Just 58000 miles!	£7000
Ford Mondeo 2 years old. 30000 miles. Alloy wheels.	£9500
Jaguar XJ6 7 years old. 1 owner. Beautiful car.	£8500

Exercise 41

Fill in an HP schedule for each of the following people who wish to buy a car from **Hunter & March.**

1. On February 4th, J Yates decides to put down a 50% deposit on the Jaguar XJ6, and pay the rest on HP over 1 year.

2. Having fallen off his motorbike yet again, K Bellett decides to buy a car. On 20th August he pays 70% deposit on the Rolls Royce Silver Shadow and decides to pay the rest over 2 years.

3. E Clark has been thinking about getting a more modern car. On June 7th, she makes up her mind and pays 40% deposit on the Ford Mondeo. The rest will be on HP over 3 years.

4. In May, F Knight has decided he could just about afford an old Cavalier. He will put down 10% deposit and pay the rest over 2 years.

CHAPTER 24

Buying a Shop

24. BUYING A SHOP

In this chapter, you are going to learn about the profit that different sorts of shops can make.

Many people in Britain buy a shop at some time in their working lives.
We are known as "A nation of shopkeepers".
Unfortunately, a lot of people lose their money because they are not careful enough when they are choosing a shop. It is very easy to look at a shop and think that it is making a lot of money when actually it is not.

For instance, if someone told you that a shop was doing a trade of £2,600 a week you might think **"Wow! £2,600 in a week!"**
But the owner of the shop could be quite poor.

You have probably heard people say: "that shop must be a goldmine" – meaning that it must make a great deal of money. It could be true. Some shops do make a lot of money. The thing is – how can you tell?

Look at the advertisement below.

> Self Service General Stores.
>
> Spac., mod., well apptd. shop sit in unopposed postn. serving a well pop.
> Rsdntl. area. Run by couple with part time help.
> Hours 8.30 am to 6 pm and 9 to 12 Sunday morning.
> s-c accom. Comp. kit. lounge/diner, 2 dbl. bdrms., bthrm. and sep WC.
> Shop has clkrm. and large stockroom.
> Takings £2600 per week. Secure lease at £4600 p.a.
> Recmd. at £65000 s.a.v.

The first thing to do is to find out what it's talking about!
Use the Shop Vocabulary below to see what everything means.

SHOP VOCABULARY

bedrm	Bedroom
bthrm	Bathroom
cabnt	Cabinet
clkrm	Cloakroom
comp	Comprising
dble	Double
d-f	Double fronted
kit	Kitchen
livrm	Living room
lu	Lock Up
mod	Modern
p.a.	per annum
preptn	Preparation
p.w.	Per week
sav	Stock at valuation
s-c accom	Self contained accommodation
sep	Separate
sit	Situated
spac	Spacious
t/o	Turnover (amount of money taken)

If you were interested in buying the shop, you would go and "view" it (look around it).
The shopkeeper would answer any questions and give you information about the cost of things.

Imagine you got the following information.

Rates £1,040 p.a.
Wages for part time help £50.
Electricity £148 a quarter.
Wrapping paper and bags £40 p.w.
Profit 20%

Now let's see how much money the shop actually makes.
£2,600 per week sounds very nice but unfortunately it is not all profit. Before the goods can be sold, the shopkeeper has to buy them from a supplier.
The goods are then sold at a higher price to make a profit – 20% in this case.

20% of £2,600 = $\frac{20}{100}$ x $\frac{2600}{1}$ = $\frac{52000}{100}$ = **£520**

£520 p.w. still sounds fairly good – but we have not finished yet.

£520 p.w. is called the **Gross** profit.
It means the profit made from selling the goods.

What we really want to know is how much profit the shop is making after ALL expenses have been taken into account
This is called the **Net** profit.

The other expenses include rent, rates, electricity, gas, wages for part time helpers and paper bags. These expenses are called **Overheads**.

Let's work out the overheads.

1. Rent is £4,602 p.a. Divide by 52 to get weekly rent. Answer **£88.50**
2. Rates are £2,080 a year. Divide by 52 to get weekly rate. Answer **£40**
3. Electricity is £156 a quarter. That means a quarter of a year which is 13 weeks. So divide by 13 to get weekly amount. Answer **£12**
4. Wages **£50**
5. Paper bags and wrapping paper **£40**

Total overheads = 88.5 + 40 + 12 + 50 + 40 = £230.50

The gross profit (money made by selling the goods) was £520.
Take away the overheads to see what the net profit is (money you have left over).

NET profit = £520 - £230.50 = **£289.50**

That's not so good is it? You haven't even paid income tax yet. Mind you, the rent rates are paid so that is something. However, it is not a great living. Especially if you consider the very long hours, early morning starts, and working Sundays as well. Even when the shop is closed, there is work to do. You have to order all the goods that you are running short of, clean the shop and keep accounts for the tax man.

Do any shops make a really good living?

Yes!

Fish and chip shops do very well.

A good pub does even better.

Exercise 42

Below are advertisements of shops for sale.
At the end of each one is information supplied by the shopkeeper.

Work out the **gross** profit, the **overheads** and the **net** profit for one week.

The figures are real and show the sort of money that the shop would be making.

1. **Fish and chips**
   Easily run shop. Take away. Good tourist trade in summer. Excellent main road pos, in thriving coastal town. Large supermarket and car park next door.
   The shop is newly fitted with a 3 pan counter range and the general décor is very attractive. Preptn rm. with chipper, peeler, 2 deep freezers and a large fish cabinet.
   Accom 3 bedrms., large lvrm., kit. Bthrm and toilet. Garage.

   Trade £3,000 p.w.
   Very good council lease at rent of just £7,540 p.a.
   Price £120,000 for quick sale.

Information supplied by shop owner.
Wages for part time help £100 p.w.
Rates £5,304 p.a.
Frying oil £190 p.w.
Gas £546 a quarter
Electricity £286 a quarter
Wrapping paper £60 p.w.
Profit 55%

2. **Greengrocers**
   Very smart shop in mod. Parade. Run by couple with 3 assistants. s-c accom. 3 bedrms., lounge, kit.,bthrm. and sep. WC. Coldroom to rear. Turnover £5380 p.w.

   Profit 26%

Information supplied by shop owner.
Rates £6032 p.a.
Rent £12012 p.a.
Wages £31044 p.a.
Electricity £481 a quarter.
Wrapping paper and bags £90 p.w.

ANSWERS

ANSWERS

Exercise 1

1
a) 1 hour. 9 hours
b) 1cm. 17cm
c) 3 cards or 3 weeks
   13 cards or 13 weeks
d) 1 second or 1 minute
   7 seconds or 7 minutes
e) 1mm 7mm
f) 11 days in Sept, April
   June or Nov

There are just possible answers. You may have slightly different answers.

2 Each week you will work 5 days, 8 hours each day with 1 hour each day for lunch.

3 20 minutes

4 70p

5 I have only got 8 cards and I should have 9 cards. Someone has got a card up their sleeve.

Exercise 2

1 110   **2** 344 feet
3 500   **4** 33 years
5 27 years   **6** 39 years
7 1000000   **8** £199.98
9 £735

Exercise 4

1 $\frac{7}{10}$ **2** $\frac{2}{3}$ **3** $\frac{5}{6}$

4 $\frac{3}{4}$ **5** $\frac{2}{5}$ **6** $\frac{3}{10}$

7 $\frac{1}{20}$ **8** $\frac{4}{15}$

Exercise 3

1 a) $\frac{1}{2}$ b) $\frac{3}{4}$ c) $\frac{1}{5}$ d) $\frac{4}{5}$ e) $\frac{2}{5}$

f) $\frac{2}{5}$ g) $\frac{3}{10}$ h) $\frac{1}{3}$ i) $\frac{3}{5}$ j) $\frac{1}{4}$

2 $\frac{75}{300} = \frac{1}{4}$ so earthworm = 4 x 1 metre = 4 metres.

3 $\frac{21}{126} = \frac{7}{42} = \frac{1}{6}$

4 $\frac{18}{150} = \frac{9}{75} = \frac{3}{25}$

5 $\frac{35}{350} = \frac{7}{70} = \frac{1}{10}$ so speed of sound = 10 x 76 = 760 mph

6 $\frac{36}{144} = \frac{18}{72} = \frac{9}{36} = \frac{1}{4}$ so pigeon speed = 4 x 15 = 60 mph

7 $\frac{15}{90} = \frac{5}{30} = \frac{1}{6}$ donation = 6 x 17000 = £102000

8 $\frac{15}{105} = \frac{5}{35} = \frac{1}{7}$ fuel = 7 x 6000 = 42000 gallons

Exercise 5

1 a) $\frac{4+3}{12} = \frac{7}{12}$ b) $\frac{9+4}{36} = \frac{13}{36}$ c) $\frac{8+7}{56} = \frac{15}{56}$ d) $\frac{5+12}{60} = \frac{17}{60}$

e) $\frac{8+4}{32} = \frac{12}{32} = \frac{3}{8}$ f) $\frac{4+11}{44} = \frac{15}{44}$ g) $\frac{2+9}{18} = \frac{11}{18}$ h) $\frac{3+10}{30} = \frac{13}{30}$

2 $\frac{1}{6} + \frac{1}{5} = \frac{5+6}{30} = \frac{11}{30}$ of an hour = 22 minutes

3 $\frac{1}{5} + \frac{1}{2} = \frac{2+5}{10} = \frac{7}{10}$ of a tonne = 700 kg

Exercise 6

1 a) $\frac{10+21}{35} = \frac{31}{35}$ b) $\frac{15+8}{24} = \frac{23}{24}$ c) $\frac{28-27}{36} = \frac{1}{36}$ d) $\frac{21-16}{24} = \frac{5}{24}$

e) $\frac{60+16}{96} = \frac{76}{96} = \frac{19}{24}$ f) $\frac{6-4}{4} = \frac{4}{4} = 1$ g) $\frac{5+2}{10} = \frac{7}{10}$

h) $\frac{15-8}{40} = \frac{7}{40}$ i) $\frac{12-5}{15} = \frac{2}{15}$ j) $\frac{35+24}{84} = \frac{59}{84}$ k) $\frac{8+6}{16} = \frac{14}{16} = \frac{7}{8}$

l) $\frac{16-7}{28} = \frac{9}{28}$ m) $\frac{55-48}{60} = \frac{7}{60}$ n) $\frac{9+7}{21} = \frac{16}{21}$ o) $\frac{15-8}{20} = \frac{7}{20}$

p) $\frac{5+8}{20} = \frac{13}{20}$

Work to mark.

a) Wrong. Should be $\frac{17}{21}$
b) Wrong. Should be $\frac{14-3}{21} = \frac{11}{21}$
c) Correct
d) Wrong. Should be $\frac{30+11}{110} = \frac{41}{110}$

Exercise 7

1 a) 0810 b) 2010 c) 1445 d) 0245 e)2220

f) 1050 g) 1055 h) 2355

2 a) 2.30 pm b) 9.35 pm c)7.45 am d) 12.01 am e) 7.20 pm

f) 5.18 am g) 4.40 pm h) 5.50 pm

Exercise 8

1 4 pm to 6 pm   **2** 1800 to 2000   **3** 0000 to 0400   **4** 2230

5 It surfaced at 1.40 am and started leaping at 2.10 am. Dived at 2.25 am

6 7   **7** 11.59 pm **8** 0840   **9** 5.35 pm   **10** 1902

Exercise 9

1 a) $\frac{15}{36}$ **b)** $\frac{3}{16}$ **c)** $\frac{8}{15}$ **d)** $\frac{12}{21} = \frac{4}{7}$

e) $\frac{6}{35}$ **f)** $\frac{35}{56} = \frac{5}{8}$

2 a) $\frac{189}{7} = 27$ **b)** $\frac{480}{12} = 40$ **c)** $\frac{392}{8} = 49$ **d)** $\frac{240}{3} = 80$

e) $\frac{264}{4} = 66$ **f)** $\frac{360}{5} = 72$

3 206 bones   **4** 80 years   **5** 30 g   **6** 59 days

Exercise 10

1 a) $\frac{1x4}{2x3} = \frac{4}{6} = \frac{2}{3}$ **b)** $\frac{5x9}{8x7} = \frac{45}{56}$ **c)** $\frac{2x5}{3x4} = \frac{10}{12} = \frac{5}{6}$ **d)** $\frac{1 \, x \, 1}{9 \, x \, 3} = \frac{1}{27}$

e) $\frac{3x1}{5x4} = \frac{3}{20}$ **f)** $\frac{3x2}{11x1} = \frac{6}{11}$ **g)** $\frac{5x4}{7x3} = \frac{20}{21}$ **h)** $\frac{7x9}{8x2} = \frac{63}{16}$

i) $\frac{6x4}{15x3} = \frac{24}{45} = \frac{8}{15}$ **j)** $\frac{7x6}{5x12} = \frac{42}{60} = \frac{21}{30} = \frac{7}{10}$

Exercise 11

a) $\frac{28}{8} = 3\frac{4}{8} = 3\frac{1}{2}$ **b)** $\frac{45}{2} = 22\frac{1}{2}$ **c)** $\frac{14}{3} = 4\frac{2}{3}$ **d)** $\frac{48}{3} = 16$

e) $\frac{34}{5} = 6\frac{4}{5}$ **f)** $\frac{17}{3} = 5\frac{2}{3}$ **g)** $\frac{54}{7} = 7\frac{5}{7}$ **h)** $\frac{26}{4} = 6\frac{2}{4} = 6\frac{1}{2}$

i) $\frac{91}{4} = 22\frac{3}{4}$ **j)** $\frac{31}{6} = 5\frac{1}{6}$

Exercise 12

1 a) $\frac{5x7}{4} = \frac{35}{4} = 8\frac{3}{4}$ b) $\frac{29x3}{8x5} = \frac{87}{40} = 2\frac{7}{40}$

   c) $\frac{23x5-8x13}{8x5} = \frac{115-104}{40} = \frac{11}{40}$ d) $\frac{11x2+6x3}{6x2} = \frac{22+18}{12} = \frac{40}{12} = 3\frac{4}{12} = 3\frac{1}{3}$

2 $\frac{5}{2} \times \frac{7}{2} = \frac{35}{4} = 8\frac{3}{4}$ gallons   3 $\frac{2}{3} \times \frac{27}{1} = \frac{54}{3}$ = 18 birds

4 $\frac{5}{4} \times \frac{22}{5} = \frac{110}{20} = 5\frac{10}{20} = 5\frac{1}{2}$ million   5 $\frac{3 \, x \, 15+1 \, x \, 5}{5 \, x \, 15} = \frac{50}{75} = \frac{10}{15} = \frac{2}{3}$

6 $\frac{11}{3} - \frac{19}{15} = \frac{11x15-3x19}{3x15} = \frac{165-57}{45} = \frac{108}{45} = 2\frac{18}{45} = 2\frac{6}{15} = 2\frac{2}{5}$ seconds

Exercise 13

1 388	**2** 62	**3** 173	**4** 128
5 2259	**6** 5024	**7** 19784	**8** 644887
9 4403776745		**10** 2488879601692	

Exercise 14

1 a) 378   b) 1292   c) 10712   d) 479682   e) 1104   f) 2948

   g) 77736 h) 932904 i) 2590   j) 7536   k)181467   l) 19615904

2 34983   3 780   4 41685   5 4999995 6 3520   7 £809600

8 7200 days: 144000 days   9 181080 days

10 524288   549755813888   11 1040465790

Exercise 15

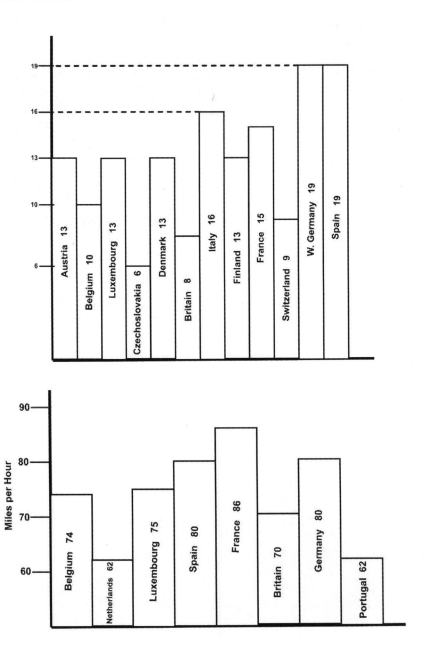

Three paragraphs.

I think it is quite obvious that paragraph 2 (below) is definitely a different shape to paragraphs 1 and 3. **Paragraphs 1 and 3 were written by the same person.**

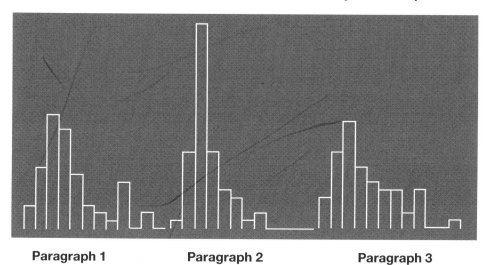

Paragraph 1   Paragraph 2   Paragraph 3

Exercise 16

1

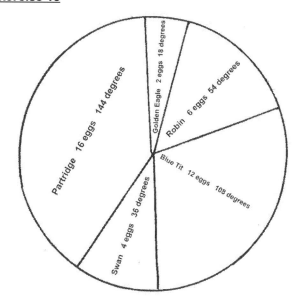

2

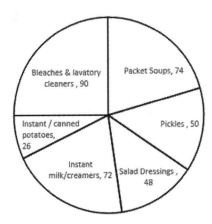

Bleaches & lavatory cleaners , 90
Packet Soups, 74
Instant / canned potatoes, 26
Pickles , 50
Instant milk/creamers, 72
Salad Dressings , 48

Exercise 17

1 a) 31.645   b) 11.173   c) 459.1244   d) 363.2
   e) 402.76   f) 51.721   g) 73.2767   h) 10.82

2 a) £358.45   b) £17.99   c) £67.15   d) £36.14
   e) £41.68   f) £274.32   g) £24.14   h) £14.25
   i) £33.14

3 73.66

4 a) 1339885.180907   b) 650854.44078

5 Added = 498723953100860.81918699827367
   Subtracted = 498723938553569.36649180648633

Exercise 18

1 Mean = 95/19 = 5. Mode = 3. Median = 5
2 Mean = 480/6 = 80. Mode = 26. Median = (28+100)/2 = 64
3 Mean = 812/7 = 116. Mode =100. Median = 100

Exercise 19

1 3 Red pencils were added so there are now 6 Red
  Needs 5 Yellow pencils to make 7 Yellow
2 They weighed 6lbs each. Total weight=7x9=63lbs.
  51 lbs accounted for so 12 to make total of 63.
  Each twin weighed the same so they weighed 6lbs each.

Exercise 20

1 a) 79p b) 21p c) £0.56

2 a) £6.24 b) £5.29 c) £5.25

3 a) £4.50 b) £4.82

4 a) £83.07 b) £39.77 c) £127.20

5 a) £1.38 b) 63p c) £1.37

6 a) £6.02 b) £5.99 c) £8.32

Exercise 21

1 £9.23 + 2x£0.92 + £0.09 = **£11.16**

Restaurant Merveilleux

Date 9th May		Francs
Consomme		16
Omelette aux champignons		58
Gâteau aux chocolat		17
Vin/verre	2 portiions	30
	Total	121

2 £4.24x7+£0.42x3+£0.04x4=£31.10

TRATTORIA VENTIMIGLIA

Date 15th July		Lire
Zuppa di cosa		5940
Calamarette alla sarda		18860
Castagnaccio	2 porzione	12040
Caffe tazza	3 porzione	3240
Minestrone alla Fiorentina		5170
Fonduta		16650
Panettone		7482
Vino/bicchiere	2 porzione	4050
	Totale	73432

3 £9.23x4 + £4.61 + £0.92x3 + 3x£0.09 = **£44.56**

Restaurant Merveilleux

Date 2nd September		Francs
Bisque de homard		30
Entrecôte		75
Riz au lait		27
Vin/verre		15
Consommé		16
Canard à l'orange		85
Macédoine de fruits		45
Café/tasse		9
Omelette aux champignons		58
Crèmes glacées	2 portions	64
Purée de tomate		27
Crèmes glacées		32
	Total	483

4 £9.23 + £4.61 + £0.92 + 2x£0.09 = **£14.94**

Restaurant Merveilleux

Date 2nd September		Francs
Escargots	2 portions	102
Vin/verre		60
	Total	162

5   17x4.24 + 8x0.42 +4x0.04 +0. 02 = **£75.62**

TRATTORIA VENTIMIGLIA

Date 7th July		Lire
Stracciatella	6 porzione	24300
Bistecca alla Fiorentina	4 porzione	67500
Cordula		8400
Fegato alla Veneziana		18920
Cassata	4 porzione	34400
Cannariculi	2 porzione	8370
Caffe/tazza	6 porzione	6480
Vino/bicchiere	5 porzione	10125
	Totale	178495

6 2x4.24+2.12+4x0.42+4x0.04 = **£15.13**

TRATTORIA VENTIMIGLIA

Date 4th December	Lire
Pizza frutti di mare	19800
Insalata di frutta	9600
Totale	29400

Exercise 22

1 24   **2** 20   **3** 85   **4** Hare = 45 mph Rhino = 35 mph

5 97   **6** Christmas Day = CUMKU 19th
                  New Year's Day = POP 1st
                  St. Valentine's Day = ZIP 5th

Exercise 23

1 26.3   **2** 28.96   **3** 194.06   **4** 22.5

5 1967.77   **6** 23   **7** 84   **8** 63

Exercise 24

1 a) 4.8   b) 17.69   c) 86.1   d) 1.872   e) 6.7232   f) 0.522

   g) 0.0005535   h) 36.038   i) 82.9917   j) 0.00000000714

Exercise 25

1. 1.3	**6.** 35.7
2. 5.2	**7.** 1.6
3. 6.7	**8.** 9.12
4. 28	**9.** 14.3
5. 3.6	**10.** 0.98

A Hollow moved the decimal point left instead of right.

The answer should be 12.4

Exercise 26

1

| 25/1 2014 | | **Multinational Bank PLC** | 25/1 2014 |
| | | Deal Branch, 117 Blenheim Road, Deal, Kent, CT14 7HA | |

Pay.... CASH .... or order

CASH   Fifteen pounds only   **£ 15.00**

S Green

£15.00   *S Green*

287135   287135   52   3029   38510091

2

| 7/5 2014 | | **Multinational Bank PLC** | 7/5 2014 |
| | | Deal Branch, 117 Blenheim Road, Deal, Kent, CT14 7HA | |

Pay.... Consolidated Credit Ltd .... or order

C Credit Ltd   Fourteen pounds 52p   **£ 14.52**

B Adamson

£14.52   *B Adamson*

336091   336091   52   3029   38510091

Bank giro credit

Date 7/5/2014

Cashier's stamp

33 – 45– 23

Multinational Bank PLC

Deal Branch

Notes	£50	
	£20	40.00
	£10	30.00
	£5	60.00
Coins	£1	6.00
	Silver	15.45
	Bronze	1.05
Total cash £		152.50
Cheques etc.		
No. of cheques etc.		
£		152.50

Paid in by
D Clough

B Adamson

55672001   33   4523

3

Bank giro credit

Date 9/8/14

Cashier's stamp

33 – 45– 23

Multinational Bank PLC

Deal Branch

Notes	£50	
	£20	80.00
	£10	60.00
	£5	55.00
Coins	£1	3.00
	Silver	9.00
	Bronze	0.64
Total cash £		207.64
Cheques etc.		58.61
No. of cheques etc. 4		
£		266.25

Paid in by
D Clough

J Yates

55672001   33   4523

Exercise 27

Customer's name   J Tanner

Date	Details		Debits	Credits	Balance
28 June	Balance forward				315.28
28 June	Cheque	446325	18.53		296.75
29 June	Cheque	446326	197.40		99.35
7 July	SO		16.00		83.35
17 July	Cheque	446331	29.34		54.01
21 July	Cheque				
1 July	Cheque	446333	8.50		45.51
21 July	Cheque	812357		450.00	495.51
25 July	Cash/Cheques			43.00	538.51

Exercise 28

1	2015	**2**	1 hour. 1819
3	15.10	**4**	5 hours 19 minutes
5	53 minutes	**6**	Holyhead to Colwyn Bay

Exercise 29

1 Flight 538. 7 hours 15 minutes
2 1420
3 2 stations. 4 hours 20 minutes
4 1222
5 528
6 1917
7 1446
8 Rhyl

Car Rallies

1	Sudbury	6	Thetford
2	Gobowen	7	Corwen
3	Fakenham	8	Fakenham
4	Llangollen	9	Cross Foxes
5	Ruthin	10	Southwold

Exercise 30

1 2 weeks   **2** 16.1 metres   **3** 170 chins   **4** 120 mph

5 760 mph   **6** 135 kg   **7** £2.48

8 a) £8.40 b) £561.60 c) £100.80

Exercise 31

1. a) 7.81   c) 34.178   e) 43.96
   b) 5.625   d) 6.035   f) 2.227

2. £90.24   3. £468

Exercise 32

HUNTER & MARCH		
GARAGE LTD		

Date 17/5/14
Customer R Darby
Address Blenheim Road

Work carried out:-	Hours	Cost
Accident repairs	40	£3600
Total labour charge		£3600

Parts and material

Front bumper	£212.00
Bonnet	£645.00
Radiator	£348.27
Radiator grille	£316.00
Front wing	£399.00
Headlamp	£231.00

Total parts cost	£2151.27
Labour plus parts	£5751.27
VAT at 20%	£1150.25
TOTAL	£6901.52

HUNTER & MARCH		
GARAGE LTD		

Date 18/5/14
Customer D Kemp
Address The Spinney

Work carried out:-	Hours	Cost
Fit exchange engine	15	£1350
Total labour charge		£1350

Parts and material

Exchange engine	£5300.00
8 spark plugs	£64.00
Oil filter	£8.00
7 litres engine oil	£112.00

Total parts cost	£5484.00
Labour plus parts	£6834.00
VAT at 20%	£1366.80
TOTAL	£8200.80

Exercise 33

1 5.5 m²　　**2** 7300 m²　　**3** 25420.8 m²　**4** 18 cm²

5 15 sq.in　　**6** 85 mm²　　**7** 36 cm²　　**8** 3650 m²

9 2　　　　**10** Did not change 50 mm to 5 cm. $\frac{63}{8} = 7\frac{7}{8}$

Exercise 34

1 806 sq ft　　**2** 362500 sq miles　**3** 14 cm²　　**4** 3 sq in

5 15 cm²　　**6** 17.5 cm²　　**7** 4 cm

8 Different possibilities for base x height: 8x6, 24x2, 48x1, 16x3

Exercise 35

1. 28.26 cm²
2. 452.16 sq ft
3. 153.86 sq miles
4. 0.785 cm²

Exercise 36

540 + 1620 + 75 + 450 + 160 + 60 + 10 + 20 = **2935 mm²**

Exercise 37

1. £420 x 2 + £60 x 2 + £98 x 2 + £62.50 x 2 = £1281
2. 4980 + 553.56 + 420 + 390 + 588 + 480 = £7411.56

Exercise 38

1 Bearing 120°. Distance 26 km

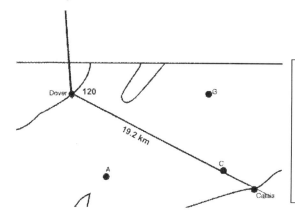

100% accuracy is NOT expected in these navigation problems because the maps are not very large.

As long as your answer is VERY close to the one given then that is fine.

2 British boat 67° for 12 km. French boat 331° for 18 km

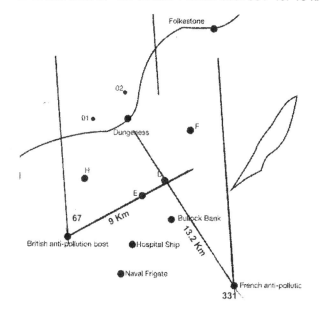

Exercise 39

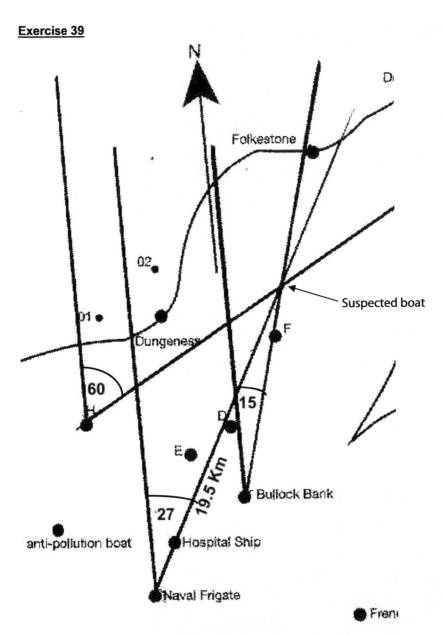

Naval frigate must sail on a bearing of 027° for a distance of 19.5 km

The Treasure Ships

1 Bearing of Carmelan from Stoura Stack is 225°

2 Bearing of Kenemerlandt from A is 103°

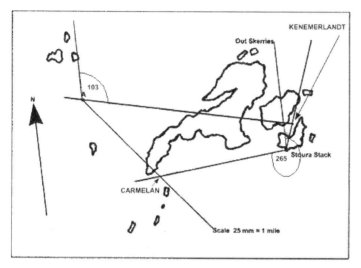

3 The Viking ships are on a bearing of 140° from Quarff

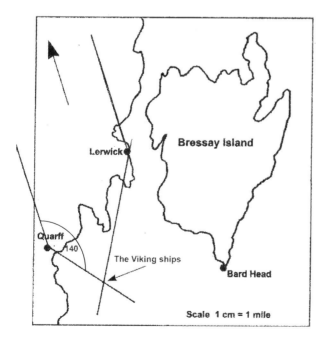

4 Bearing from Montieth is 155°

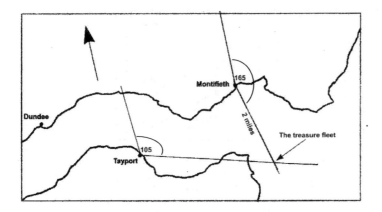

5 Bearing from St. Nicholas = 035°

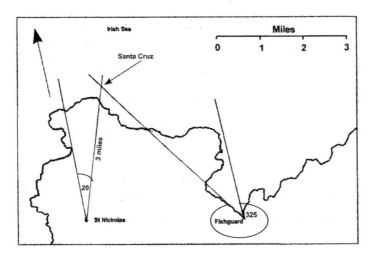

6 Bearing from Urie Ness = 126°

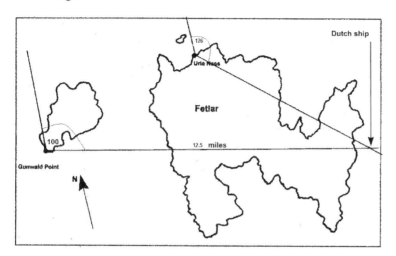

Exercise 40

	Deposit	Balance	Interest	Installments
1.	£84	£336	£40.32x2 = £80.64	£17.36
2.	£81	£459	£55.08x3 = £165.24	£17.34
3.	£126	£1134	£136.08x3 = £408.24	£42.84
4.	£108	£252	£30.24x2 = £60.48	£13.02

Exercise 41

1

```
                        SCHEDULE

Vehicle          Age              Model
Jaguar           7 Years          XJ6

Name of purchaser    J Yates


        Cash price               £ 8500
        Deposit                  £ 4250
        Balance                  £ 4250
        Interest                 £ 467.50

        balance + interest       £ 4717.50
        HP Term                  Years  1
        Monthly installments     £ 393.12


First payment due on 1st day of   March
```

2

```
                        SCHEDULE

Vehicle          Age              Model
Rolls Royce      42 Years         Silver Shadow

Name of purchaser    K Bellett


        Cash price               £ 7000
        Deposit                  £ 4900
        Balance                  £ 2100
        Interest                 £ 462

        balance + interest       £ 2562
        HP Term                  Years  2
        Monthly installments     £ 106.75


First payment due on 1st day of   September
```

3

SCHEDULE

Vehicle	Age	Model
Ford	2 Years	Mondeo

Name of purchaser   E Clark

Cash price	£ 9500
Deposit	£ 3800
Balance	£ 5700
Interest	£ 1368
balance + interest	£ 7068
HP Term	Years 3
Monthly installments	£ 196.33

First payment due on 1st day of   July

4

SCHEDULE

Vehicle	Age	Model
Vauxhall	18 Years	Cavalier

Name of purchaser   F Knight

Cash price	£ 650
Deposit	£ 65
Balance	£ 585
Interest	£ 128.70
balance + interest	£ 713.70
HP Term	Years 2
Monthly installments	£ 29.73

First payment due on 1st day of   June

Exercise 42

1. **Gross Profit** = 55% of £3000 = **£1650** per week
    Overheads
    a) Rent £145   b) Wages £100   c) Rates £102   d) Oil £190
    e) Gas £46   f) Electricity £23   g) Wrapping paper £60
    Total overheads = £661
    Net profit = £1650 – £984 = **£666**

2. **Gross profit** = 26% of £5380 = £1398.80
    Overheads
    a) Rent £231   b) Rates £116   c) £597   d) Electricity £40
    e) Wrapping paper and bags £90
    Total overheads = £1074
    Net profit = £1398.80 – £1074 = **£324.80**

A FEW FINAL WORDS...

You have now reached the end of your Maths is Easy guide. No doubt that you feel more comfortable and confident with these tests and will be able to successfully pass any Mathematical test.

For any mathematical test, there are a few things to remember to help you perform at your best:

REMEMBER – The THREE P's!

1. **Prepare.** This may seem relatively obvious, but you will be surprised how many people fail mathematical testing because they lacked knowledge and understanding of what to expect. Be sure to practice these tests before having to sit a real test. Not only will you become familiar with the testing questions, it will also take off some of the pressure leading up to that all important test. Like anything, the more you practice, the more likely you are to succeed!

2. **Perseverance.** You are far more likely to succeed at something if you continuously set out to achieve it. Everybody comes across times where they are set back or find obstacles in the way of their goals. The important thing to remember when this happens, is to use those setbacks and obstacles as a way of progressing. It is what you do with your past experiences that helps to determine your success in the future. If you fail at something, consider 'why' you have failed. This will allow you to improve and enhance your performance for the next time.

3. **Performance.** Performance is a great word. Your performance will determine whether or not you are likely to succeed. Attributes that are often associated with performance are self-belief, motivation and commitment. Self-belief is important for anything you do in your life. It allows you to recognise your own abilities and skills and believe that you can do well. Believing that you can do well is half the battle! Being fully motivated and committed is often difficult for some people, but we can assure you that, nothing is gained without hard work and determination. If you want to succeed, you will need to put in that extra time and hard work!

Good luck with your Mathematical Tests. We wish you the best of luck with all your future endeavours!

The how2become team

The How2Become Team

how2become

Get more books, manuals, online tests
and training courses at:

www.How2Become.com

Printed in Great Britain
by Amazon